SERVING AS SENDERS

D1043529

SERVING AS SENDERS

HOW TO CARE FOR YOUR MISSIONARIES

NEAL PIROLO

OM
publishing

Originally published 1991 by Emmaus Road, International, Inc.,
7150 Tanner Court, San Diego, CA 92111, U.S.A.

This revised edition first published 1997 by OM Publishing

Reprinted 1999

03 02 01 00 99   7 6 5 4 3 2

OM Publishing is an imprint of Paternoster Publishing,
P.O. Box 300, Carlisle, Cumbria, CA3 OQS, U.K.

British Library Cataloguing in Publication Data

A catalogue record for this book is available from the British Library

ISBN 1-85078-199-0

Typeset by WestKey Ltd, Falmouth, Cornwall
Printed in Great Britain by Mackays of Chatham PLC, Chatham, Kent

Dedication

To the many
cross-cultural workers
and their support teams
out of whose experiences
come the pages of this book.

Serving as Senders is formatted for individual and group study. The eight study sessions have sections on:

- *For Your Personal Involvement*
- *Action steps*
- *Group Discussion*
- *For Further Action*

Contents

Acknowledgements

Who would have thought such a little book would bring such labour? Yet who would have thought of the joy it also brings? The coaching team was great! The first acknowledgement must go to the Holy Spirit, our inspiration and comfort. Second, to my wife Yvonne who often critiqued and rewrote so forcefully that I tried to get her name on the cover. To my brother Paul who didn't laugh when he read through the first draft and used his editing skills to meticulously comb through the final manuscript. To Alice Lovas who co-ordinated and wrote much of the Sacramento church's case study. To the friends of El Adobe Trust who funded the first printing. And even to our kids, for, as our son Byron pointed out, our experiences in raising them have built into us what it took to stay with this project to its completion!

And finally and foremost, 'to him who is able to do immeasurably more than all we ask or imagine . . . to him be glory . . . throughout all generations' (Ephesians 3:20, 21).

Preface

I sat in the upper level of the auditorium at the University of Illinois in Urbana, listening to the heavy-weights of the evangelical community challenge 17,000 college students to a vital and personal commitment to world evangelization. It was InterVarsity's Urbana Student Mission Conference.

I must admit I had begun daydreaming when all of a sudden there was that statement: 'In secular war, for every one person on the battle front, there are *nine* others backing him up in what is called the "line of communication." '

The concept exploded like a mortar shell! The speaker had been drawing a parallel between secular war and the spiritual warfare that accompanies cross-cultural ministry. He continued, 'And how can we expect to win with any less than that ratio? God is not looking for Lone Rangers or superstars; he is commanding an army—soldiers of the cross.'

I said, 'Thank you, Lord, for that confirmation!' At that time I was directing a one-year school of evangelism which had a strong emphasis on cross- cultural outreach. Though I had had no background in secular war, as soon as students applied to the school, I had been encouraging them to build around themselves a team of *nine* people who would support them in prayer, since enrolling in this school was saying to the enemy, 'I am getting out of the *pew* and onto the *battlefield!*'

Since that evening at Urbana, with more vigour than ever, I have encouraged, exhorted—even implored—anyone going into cross-cultural outreach ministry not to leave home without a strong, committed support team—a group that accepts the ministry of serving as senders.

By the time we have finished with our study together, you'll be able to answer this question: How can I get involved in the Great Commission of world evangelization even though I'm just an ordinary human being called to stay at home?

You can become personally involved as a sender in the mission process.

Ministering by His grace,
Neal Pirolo,
San Diego, California

Chapter One

The Need for Senders

'And how can they preach unless they are sent?'

Romans 10:15

'Beth! Wake up! Please, Beth! Wake up!' Beth's room-mate held the empty Valium bottle in her hand and knew Beth wouldn't wake up. But her instinct told her to get help. The people in the next apartment helped her carry Beth to the car. A mile that seemed half way round the world brought them to the hospital. They pumped Beth's stomach. She stirred and opened her eyes.

Months later Beth could talk about it:

'I had had a normal life before this. Friends, a loving family, a good church life. Basically, I was a happy person. I had been a professional for ten years. I had held reputable positions. I had managed people. And I had managed myself quite well . . . until this.

'I had just returned from a six-month missionary venture in the Far East. My feelings were running rampant. Nostalgia flooded me as I remembered the good times; nightmares and flashbacks haunted me in the quiet solitude of night. Nobody was interested; nobody had time to hear what I had to say.

'I had just come from a fruitful experience as an administrative assistant in a medical clinic. Dumped back into the busy lifestyle of metropolitan Washington, D.C., I lost all sense of identity. Deepening feelings of isolation caused me to withdraw all the more.

'I thought if I got back into my work I could refocus my life. But the emotional instability mounted. One nightmare kept recurring:

'We had been in a village doing some medical work. Through the thundering of a tropical storm, I awoke to the sound of gunfire. Before I could go back to sleep, I saw them dragging the body of a man past the doorway of my hut. The story was that he had been caught in the fields stealing opium.

'Now back in D.C., I would awaken at night to the sounds in my brain of the *pow-pow* of the guns. And the whole ugly scene would flash through my mind again. I began using tranquillizers to control my instability. But before seven or eight in the evening, I was lost in anxiety, confusion, uncertainty—crying uncontrollably.

'Conversely, I also had a sense of "special" knowledge. I was fulfilled by a good missionary experience. Hadn't I *been there*? Hadn't I been successful? Hadn't I bonded with and nurtured Billy to health?

'We had been on our way home from some medical work in the hill country. Along the trail I stumbled on this three-month-old infant. His hands and feet were bound together with rope. He was addicted to opium. He was almost dead. We inquired as best we could whose son he was. His mother already had four children under the age of five.

'The man who was thought to be the father was away on 'business' three to four weeks at a time. It was probably this woman who had left him there to die. A couple of hundred yards away was an abandoned hut. We said we would wait there until night time to talk to his mother. She never came. At the clinic we were able to give him the care he needed. We called him Billy, and he was eventually adopted by a local Christian doctor.

'I became hyper-vigilant about this great need out there. I felt a lot of anger towards people who wouldn't let me talk about my experiences. My pastor wouldn't let me share at church. No Sunday school class had the time for me. My parents couldn't show enough interest even to look at my pictures. I became judgemental and condemning: "How can you be thinking about buying a new car when there are such great needs out there?" But I couldn't say any of that out loud. Hurt, fear, anger and guilt all turned inwards in severe depression. I couldn't sleep at night; I couldn't get out of bed in the morning. I left my job. I took more and more tranquillizers. *I just wanted somebody to acknowledge that I was back home!*

'One Sunday morning after church, I gathered the strength to go again to my pastor and say, "I am at the end of my tether! I think I'm losing it! I need your help!" With his arm around me, he said, "Beth, I am busy. I am so tied up this week. But if you must, call my office to set an appointment for a week from Wednesday. Beth, if you would just get into the Word more. . . ."

'Through the dazed fog of an existence I had been living in, all of a sudden it became crystal clear: "Pastor, I'm not worth your time!" I had made other desperate calls to various counsellors. One guy tried to date me. A psychiatrist had given my condition a fancy label. But now it was clear: "I'm not worth anybody's time!"

'I decided to take the rest of the bottle of Valium.'

It would astound most Christians to hear missionaries honestly express their desperate need for support in one area or another. Most pleas aren't as dramatic as Beth's.

But each speaks of a personal need for those who will come alongside them and serve as senders.

Mission does not just focus on those who go. Those who serve as senders are equally significant.

A Biblical Foundation

If anybody knew about going on missionary journeys *and* needing a support team, it was the apostle Paul. He said, '. . . and how can they preach unless they are *sent?*' In Romans chapter ten, he established the vital importance of cross-cultural outreach on these two levels of involvement: *Those who go and those who serve as senders*.

Paul first quoted Joel: 'Everyone who calls on the name of the Lord will be saved.' Then, in clear linear logic so well understood by the Roman mind, he appealed: 'How, then, can they call on the one they have not believed in? And how can they believe in the one of whom they have not heard?'

Today's estimate is that 2.5 billion people have not had a culturally relevant presentation of the gospel.

'And how can they hear without someone preaching to them?' Yes, there must be a 'preacher'—the missionary, the cross-cultural worker, the *one who goes*. By whatever name and by whatever means he or she gets there, there must be a proclaimer of the good news. God chose it to be this way.

Today's estimate is that there are worldwide 285,250 career missionaries and 180,000 short-term missionaries.

But wait. There is one more question in this series: 'And how can they preach unless they are *sent?*' (Rom. 10:13–15). Paul acknowledged that there are others besides those who go who must be involved in this worldwide evangelization endeavour: those who are serving as senders.

Those who go and those who serve as senders are like two units on the same cross-cultural outreach team. Both are equally important. Both are vitally involved in the fulfilment of the Great Commission. Both are dynamically integrated and moving toward the same goal. And both are assured success, for those in God's work are on the winning team!

From the humble beginnings of one hundred young people at the Mount Hermon Meeting of 1886, the Student Volunteer Movement identified and fielded over 20,000 men and women to be *goers*—ones set apart to declare the gospel and teachings of Christ to a lost and dying world.

This same movement mobilized an army of over 80,000 mission–minded people who pledged themselves to stay at home and support those who went.

In the past, many people grew up in mission–minded churches. Men and women from faraway places came to speak of the challenge to follow in their steps. Most of the time it was easy to understand that the two squads on the missionary team were *those who go* and *those who say, 'Goodbye!'*

Maybe some people in your fellowship want to be involved in world evangelization but don't feel called to go right now. The good news is there's more they can do than just say goodbye!

There is a tremendous need for *senders*. And the need goes far beyond the traditional token involvement of attending a farewell party or writing out a cheque to a missionary society. A cross-cultural worker needs the support of a team of people while they are preparing to go, while they are on the field and when they return home.

A careful reading of Paul's missionary letters will reveal how much time he spent talking to his support team—those who were involved with him in the ministry. Sometimes he complimented them, sometimes he expressed his loneliness in being away from them, sometimes he exhorted and challenged them. But he always thanked God for them.

A support team of senders is just as critical to a missionary today. Let's look at some very good reasons why.

A Cross-Cultural Worker's Life Time-line

Consider this diagram of the physical / emotional / mental / spiritual life time-line of a cross-cultural worker during their missionary experience.

A. *"Normal" Living*

The horizontal line of this diagram represents the 'normal living' base line of your missionary's existence before he

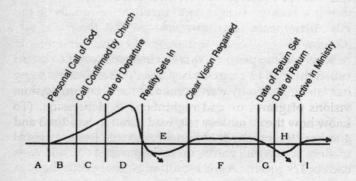

A Cross-Cultural Worker's Life Time-line

or she even had a thought about missions. This is not to say that life was flat! There were the usual ups and downs, but for the purpose of comparison, consider the line as the *normal* life before missions.

The line resembling the dips and curves of a roller-coaster ride represents the changing pulse of your missionary's being in passing through a missionary experience. One veteran said about the ups and downs of missionary life: 'Missionary living takes me on a trip that is totally outside the realm of every comfort zone I have come to enjoy!'

The vertical lines indicate periods of time, mile-stones along the missionary venture. The relative spaces between the lines may vary owing to many factors. But these are expected phases of which you, his support person, should be aware. As you are giving your support, anticipate the next mile-stone of your cross-cultural worker's life time-line. And be available to offer your assistance.

B. Anticipation of Approval

At some point, your missionary friend announced, boldly or with some reluctance, that he or she believed God had called them to be a missionary. Every fibre of their being has undergone a rise in excitement and apprehension, visions of grandeur and nightmares of depression. (To know how they probably felt, read through Exodus 3 and 4 to hear the patriarch Moses rehearse his five excuses of inadequacy. While you're there, notice that God answers each of his protests with his all–sufficiency.)

C. Anticipation of Departure

The day finally comes: The church, missionary society or other responsible body (see Acts 13:1–4) has confirmed that personal call with their approval. It has been determined that your missionary is really going! Through days, weeks, even months of preparation, support-team building, and training, anticipation heightens as the date of departure draws near.

D. Honeymoon Period

Your missionary is catapulted into space in a jet aircraft but his or her emotions are flying ten feet above the plane. The 'honeymoon' has begun. For a period of time he or she moves around in a protective bubble, enjoying the novelty of a new life. Even the single control on the shower that produces only cold water is 'interesting.' There is so much to observe, to take in. It's all so . . . different!

E. Culture Shock

The time that passes between these identified stages will vary according to circumstances. But as surely as night follows day, the next stage is inevitable. One morning your missionary rudely awakens to the reality that the single control will *never* produce hot water! They realize they are committed to circumstances that are no longer quaint; they are now *weird*, even *barbaric!*

The adventure of discovery has turned to the dread of 'What next?' The first attack of dysentery keeps him up all night. The fact that this is the most difficult language in the world to learn has her looking for a permanent interpreter. The first hints of persecution or the awareness that people are not going to change as easily or as rapidly as they had hoped have them asking God to 'Let this cup pass from me. . . .' From the pinnacles of ecstasy they have plummeted to the depths of despair. Culture stress has set in. (See pp145ff, 211.)

Most missionaries don't want to talk about this stage of missionary life because people at home won't think of them as 'spiritual' enough if they admit to some of these trying times. It is at this time that your cross-cultural worker needs your support. Many—too many—crash here. Of course, some turn back before they leave the airport!

F. Ministry of Love

But your missionary has been taught that culture shock is a normal stage to go through. Therefore, they will do just that: go through it into a time of ministry motivated by the love of Christ. Because of your strong support they will emerge with a strengthened vision of God's purposes in their life and their reasons for being a missionary. All is not rosy. The adversaries are there. But the 'great door for effective work' that Paul talked about is there, too (see 1 Cor. 16:9).

G. Anticipation of Return

Life goes on. As surely as this missionary journey had a starting point, the time will come when your cross-cultural worker will, like Paul's team, return 'to Antioch, where they had been committed to the grace of God for the work they had now completed' (Acts 14:26).

Again, feelings are mixed. Yes, your missionary wants to come home to see you. But he has made new friends. She has new ideas and ideals. He has different behaviour patterns that he knows will be difficult to integrate into his new home environment. No, she isn't returning to her old home environment when she comes back. For you also have changed!

Your missionary's heart has been broken with compassion for the lost; and there are so few to fill that empty

place in ministry. The desire to stay and continue in ministry usually out-weighs the desire to return home. Thus,
the emotional/psychological/ spiritual pulse of your missionary drops again.

Probably the shortest letter ever written was to a missionary whose furlough had been booked; all plans had
been set. Then, remembering the difficulties of previous
times at home, he wrote that he had changed his mind; he
was not coming. The reply came back: 'Pete! come home!'
He came and his support team was able to help him
through the next stage.

H.   Culture Stress in Reverse

In Chapter Seven, we deal extensively with the support
your cross-cultural worker needs after their return. The
trauma during re-entry is intense. An example is the re-entry desperation of Beth who told her story at the beginning
of this chapter. In this great time of need, your missionary
might feel especially inadequate to do any thing about it.

During this time of reverse culture stress, coming home
requires strong support.

I.   Full Integration

A missionary who has been trained to anticipate the stress
of coming home and has a strong re-entry support team
will, in time, fully integrate their changed self into the
changed home environment. They will be a positive agent
for change in their church and community, will stay 'a long
time with the disciples' (Acts 14:28), will, like Paul, remain
'in Antioch', teaching and preaching (Acts 15:35). And who
knows? After a while they might even say, 'Hey, Barnabas,
let's go out again!' (See Acts 15:36.)

Today no cross-cultural worker should leave home without a strong, integrated, educated, knowledgeable, excited-as-he-is, active team of people who have committed themselves to the work of serving as senders.

You may be a part of that team. Your heart is stirred by people of other cultures, yet you have not heard God's call to go. When a missionary speaks at your church or a breakthrough is reported, there is a quickening of your pulse. Yet you know God has directed you to stay at home. You may be called to the ministry of serving as a sender.

Prayerfully consider serving as a sender in one or more of six areas of support:

Moral Support—just 'being there'
Logistics Support—all the bits and pieces
Financial Support—money, money, money
Prayer Support—spiritual warfare at its best
Communication Support—letters, tapes and more
Re-entry Support—more than applauding
          the safe landing of a jumbo jet

Each area has its unique responsibilities; each is best served by specific gifts within the body of Christ. Allow his Spirit to speak to your heart about your possible involvement in one of these phases of support.

God's *call* on your life to serve as a sender must be just as vibrant as the call on the life of the one you send. Likewise, the *commitment* you make must be as sure as that of your cross-cultural worker. The responsible *action* you take is as important as the ministry your field worker undertakes.

And the *reward* of souls for God's kingdom will be equal to your missionary's faithfulness and your own.

A Case Study in Support

As a church in Sacramento, California began preparations to send their second missionary family, the concept of the church serving as senders became a priority. Seven couples committed themselves to direct the support team for Lou and Sandy and their six-month-old baby girl Marlies.

Each one on the team was encouraged to consider the responsibilities of each area of support. One of the team members tells the story:

> Lou and Sandy invited nine couples to their home in June. They had already been to the Philippines. They had visited several ministries there—trusting that the Lord would show them where he wanted them to serve.
> At the June meeting, Lou shared with us the opportunity they sensed God had provided for them. 'But', he said, 'the only way we will be able to go is if we have a core group responsible for our support.' He discussed the basic needs for moral, logistics, financial, prayer, communication and re-entry support and how the core group would head up each of these areas. He then asked us to pray seriously about being a part of this team effort. He wanted our answer within two weeks. As it turned out, seven couples felt God's calling to serve. That was our beginning.
> We all knew we wanted to support Lou and Sandy. After all, we had said we would be a part of the core group. But what was next? As Lou had asked George and me to head up the core group, we phoned the others to see if there was any specific area of ministry they would like to be involved in. The Hughes would head the logistics support. The Huffmans had a heart for re-entry. The Martins wanted to be responsible for communication support. Others responded in turn.
> We had our first real meeting as a core group in August. At first I think we wanted to appear as if we had 'got it all

together'. As the meeting progressed, however, it became apparent that in fact we hadn't. But praise God, the barriers began to break down and we were able to admit that we were confused in some areas. As a group we began to discuss our problems and to explore possible answers.

So here's an opportunity for you to serve as a sender, to be a vital part of the mission process.

Hang on! As we'll see in the next chapter, there's more to it than raising your hand to volunteer. As your cross-cultural worker encounters difficulties, your *moral* support is needed to protect them.

(In addition to the following individual study, see the **Group Leader's Guide** for session one beginning on page 182.)

For Your Personal Involvement

Throughout this study you will find many Scripture references. To benefit more fully from the lessons, read each one in its full context. Allow the Holy Spirit to 'guide you into all truth' (John 16:13).

□ Read Romans 10:13–15. From that passage fill in the blanks in the following statement. Notice that there is a key word in each question that leads you to the next question. The foundation of the whole sequence, then, lies in the final word!

10:13 Everyone who _____ on the name of the Lord will be saved. (See Joel 2:32.)

10:14 How, then, can they _____ on the one they have not _____ ? And how can they _____ in the one of whom

they have not _____ ? And how can they _____ without
_____ ?

10:15 And how can they _____ unless they are _____ ?
(Write that final word in capital letters to high-light in your
mind the importance of serving as senders!)

☐ List the nine stages of the physical / emotional / psychological / spiritual life time-line of a missionary, and the incident in
time that forms the transition from one to another. (See the
example on p. 7 and subheadings pp. 6–11.)

Period A:	'Normal Living';	personal call
Period B:	_____;	_____
Period C:	_____;	_____
Period D:	_____;	_____
Period E:	_____;	_____
Period F:	_____;	_____
Period G:	_____;	_____
Period H:	_____;	active in ministry
Period I:	_____;	

☐ Read the following passages relating to Paul's need
for a support team. Write in each space the type of support
Paul was either asking for or expressing thanks for: moral,
logistics, financial, prayer, communication or re-entry.
(Each area is referred to in at least one passage.)

- Ephesians 6:18–19 _____
- 2 Timothy 4:13 _____
- Acts 14:26–28 _____
- Acts 21:12–13 _____
- Romans 16 _____
- Philippians 4:10–12 _____

Read 1 Corinthians 3:4–9; 12:12–27; Revelation 2:6,15. (Some scholars believe the 'teaching of the Nicolaitans made a distinction between 'clergy' and 'laity', i.e. ordinary Christians.)

After prayer, fill in the following sentence:

In God's global plan

I,_____,

your name .

as a sender,
am as important as,
(but not more
important than)

_____

name a famous missionary
even though my role won't seem as dramatic.

Maybe you don't feel able to fill that in just now. Go ahead and read through *Serving As Senders*. By the end of our study, we trust you *will* be able to make that statement personal!

Action Steps
By the time you have read Chapter One, completed the *For Your Personal Involvement* section and participated in a group discussion (See **Group Leaders' Guide** beginning on page 182), you should . . .

- Be aware of the need for those who serve as senders.
- Explore further to know where you might fit in.

- Take the initiative. Let your missionary friend know that you are learning about the ministry of serving as a sender. And you will soon be available to help support him or her in one or more areas for God's glory!
- Involve others. Look among your fellowship for those who seem to be at a loose end. Possibly they are the cross-cultural parts of your church. Invite them to read and study this book with you.

Chapter Two

Moral Support

'Be strong and courageous. Do not be terrified; do not be discouraged, for the Lord your God will be with you wherever you go.'

Joshua 1:9

'It was a bit unusual. The rapid sequence of events, that is. We trained others to assume our ministries in the church, got married, attended a 12-week field training course in Tijuana, Mexico, and spent our first year together living on a kibbutz in Israel!

'But why not? We were young, adventurous and had not yet accumulated a lot of possessions. And most of all, the church where we had been ministering for the past three years was totally supportive. It was a small fellowship in a small town, so everyone knew us. The smiles and hugs on Sunday morning said to us, "Scott and Jean, this is right!" Deep in our own hearts, God's peace said, "This is right!"

'Invitations to our wedding included a note saying "No gifts, please; we are going to Israel!" "This is right!" they said with their donations of money instead. A prayer of blessing by our pastor at the wedding said, "This is right!" Even our non- Christian parents said, "This is right!" The moral support from every quarter said, "This is right!"

'We began our training in Tijuana. We met our Mexican host family. Classes began. Learning how to relate to each other—we had been married just four weeks—was the subject of one of the classes. We did our field work in the community, grappling with cultural adaptation and relating to our host family with our limited Spanish. But with their patience and a lot of humour, we learned how to learn a second language and we bonded with them. Principles of spiritual warfare were preparing us for battle. We were learning how to live and minister in a second culture. Communication from our home church assured us that the sense of God's direction was solid. "This is right," we said to each other.

'Then, as a part of our training to make sure the support system was "up and running," we were sent home for a long weekend. We sat in the pastor's living room. Somehow there was an awkwardness. We glanced at each other: "This is not right!" we thought.

'Then Pastor Joe spoke: "Scott and Jean, I have made the decision that you are not to continue in this mission!"

'We were stunned. Our objections were not too well thought-out and they probably didn't make much sense since we were so confused. My wife started crying. Pastor Joe said firmly, "Jean, I am not moved by your tears!" We were speechless! We became angry but he remained firm: "You are not to go! If you continue, you are on your own!"

'We were dazed. The bottom had just fallen out of our world. The whole basis of our support team was shattered! There was a very empty feeling in the pit of our stomachs. We could hardly go to church. We weren't allowed to contact any of the people there for further support. "This is not right!" we knew.

'Fortunately, a part of our support team was made up of individuals from several other churches and Bible study groups. As we all beseeched the Lord for his direction in this new situation, we came to believe that it wasn't that we shouldn't go, but that we were losing a vital part of our support team.

'Just before leaving for Israel, by chance we met Pastor Joe downtown. He was so convinced that God had spoken to him that he said if we continued on this venture, something bad was going to happen to us in Israel. He would stake his ministry on it!

'Needless to say, this added insult to injury. Not only had we lost a strong foundation of moral support, but now this prediction was to cause a continual cloud of apprehension during our whole trip. When anything risky or unknown loomed ahead, we would remember his statement. For example, one night at the kibbutz, we were awakened by a loud siren. We were ready to run for the bomb shelter as we had often practised. "This is it! What bad thing is going to happen to us?" we thought. But since we saw no one else running and the siren stopped, we went back to bed.

'The next day we discovered that the temperature in the turkey house had fallen below a safe level. The siren was to alert the men responsible to adjust the thermostat! Though the humour of that situation mellowed our apprehension, Pastor Joe's 'cloud of doom' hovered above every crisis.

'We have now returned home. It was a successful time of ministry in Israel. We're finding that God is slowly healing our relationships with the people of that church. Pastor Joe did not leave his ministry—in fact, he recently allowed us to share in a local outreach from his church!'

Moral support is the very foundation of the support system. Everyone in the church can be involved in this part of the ministry since in its most basic concept, moral support is simply saying, 'God bless you! We are excited with you in your missionary venture!'

Did the great men and women of the Bible need moral support? Let's look at a few of them.

But David Found Strength in the Lord

Jesse's seven other sons had been rejected. For 'the Lord does not look at the things man looks at. Man looks at the outward appearance, but the Lord looks at the heart.' There remained one—a boy. A teenager. They brought him in from the fields where he was tending the sheep. And the Lord said, 'Rise and anoint him; he is the one.' And the Spirit of the Lord was on David from that day forward.

Through the battle with Goliath, through the struggle with Saul's insane jealousy, through the war of nerves during the months and years of fleeing and being pursued by a king who was troubled by an evil spirit, through the conflict involved in building his royal entourage of six hundred ruthless men, the Spirit of the Lord was upon David. (See 1 Sam. 27:1–12.)

And as the Philistines were assembled against Israel, David and his men were with them. But a distrust of these Hebrews troubled the minds of the Philistines. (See 1 Sam. 29.) David and his men were sent back to Ziklag—only to discover that the Amalekites had invaded from the south, burned the city and carried away all their wives and children. And they wept 'until they had no strength left to weep . . . David was greatly distressed because the men were talking of stoning him. But David found strength in the Lord' (see 1 Samuel 30).

Imagine the intensity of the moment—the physical distress of a three-day return march to Ziklag. The adrenalin flow building up to a battle against Israel and then the let-down. The bombarding emotions of losing family and possessions. The internal battle of 'Lord, I am your anointed king of Israel. When am I going to possess the throne?' Where was David's moral support team? They wanted to stone him!

But David found strength in the Lord.

The Hour has Come

Eleven hundred years later. Another man, another occasion. He says to his three-man support team, 'My soul is overwhelmed with sorrow to the point of death. Stay here and keep watch with me' (Matt. 26:38). And now the God–man, the propitiation for our sins, 'the Lamb slain from the creation of the world' enters the most significant arena of battle of all time.

The battle of wills rages. All his humanness rises to say, 'Father, there must be another way. I cannot drink this cup of separation. We have been eternally One. Isn't there another way to redeem Man back to You? Let this cup pass from me!'

The anguish becomes intense, for he knows there is no other way. The mental and spiritual suffering of the incarnate God in atonement for the sins of fallen man leads him to the extreme of physical torture: the bloody sweat.

'Could you not keep watch with me for one hour?' Jesus questioned his followers. Twice and then a third time, he came to them: 'The hour has come!'

In each of these situations there were those who could have been supportive. But David's men, so overcome by their own loss of wives and children and homes, thought only to stone David. Christ's men, self-indulgent in sleep, were not even aware of their Master's passion that night.

What of the others? When Mary was pregnant by the Holy Spirit, Joseph's first response was to 'put her away privately'. In John 9, Jesus compassionately healed a blind man. When the Jewish elders wanted the parents' testimony in support of their son's healing, in fear they said, 'Ask him! He's old enough to tell you!' When Paul was determined to go to Jerusalem, people at two different times tried to dissuade him—even insisting that the Holy Spirit had instructed them to warn him.

The pages of history do not paint a brighter picture. Through the centuries, the pattern has not changed. Read in Ruth Tucker's biographical history of Christian missions, about the bold men and women God told to go to the nations (*From Jerusalem to Irian Jaya*—see 'Resources', page 201). You can count on the fingers of one hand the few who found strong moral support for their pioneer vision.

An English cobbler named William Carey struggled in the 1790s with the church's responsibility to the Great Commission. Later he was to become known as the 'Father of Modern Missions.' But in his early days as the vision stirred deep in his heart, there was no support. His fellow churchmen openly rebuked him by saying, 'When God pleases to convert the heathen, he will do it without your aid or ours.' His wife initially refused to join him on his voyage to India. Only a delay in the departure date gave her the opportunity to reconsider.

Today as thousands of cross-cultural workers grapple with the issues of being 'soldiers of the cross' in another culture, what sort of moral support can they anticipate from people?

- People so lost in their own narrow world that they do not support God's anointed but rather begin hurling stones of incrimination—like David's men?
- People lulled into self-indulgent sleep to such an extent that they are unaware of God's plan for their friends—like Christ's men?
- People so concerned about public opinion that they want to nod nicely at missionary zeal but try to send their worker away privately—like Joseph?
- People so afraid for the other programmes of their church that they don't want anything to do with daring adventures into the unknown, the uncomfortable? Mission ministry, after all, could be regarded as competition to the status quo—according to moral-non-supporters like the Jewish elders?
- People so sure they have 'heard from the Lord' that the missionary's 'hearing from the Lord' is wrong?
- People who pierce God's missionary heart by distorting their theology—like Carey's friends?

Stones for Building — or Throwing

Stones of incrimination. Some people cannot handle the personal challenge presented by a friend who thinks God wants her to do such a bold, daring thing as go to the mission field. Whether ignorantly, out of well-meaning friendship or to assuage their own feelings of distress, they may begin hurling stones of incrimination: 'But it's a rough world out there! Riots and wars! Hatred and violence! You could get yourself killed!'

Other insensitive responses might include, 'You must be joking! You? A missionary? What do you think you can do to save the world?'

Often close, loving friends counsel:

- You're needed here. You have so much to offer right here in our fellowship.
- Waste your education out in the middle of nowhere? What will your parents say?
- Why don't you get a real job? Make some money so you'll be secure; later on you can think about getting involved in missions.
- You can't upset your mother like this. How can you take her grandchildren away from her? They need her!
- What about your kids' education? They will come home ignoramuses and social misfits!
- You expect to get married out there? You'll never meet anybody!

In a final lament, abandoning all logic, they may cry, 'I don't believe this is happening to me!'

The cross-cultural worker who has already battled it out with the Lord over feelings of inadequacy sits in a dishevelled heap—beneath a pile of stones, battered and hurting. The few and the strong who make it find strength in the Lord. But it would be so much better if they had you as a part of their Moral Support Team to encourage them.

Self-indulgent sleep is the state of too large a section of today's church. Self-indulgence has produced a myopic introspection; we seem to focus on healing ourselves so we can have nicer lives. 'Lord, comfort me so that I will be comfortable' is in direct contrast to what is told the church in 2 Corinthians 1:4.

We want to be comfortable and we want security. We feel uneasy about unpredictability—like Peter as he blurted out, in his threatened loss of security, 'Never, Lord! . . . This shall never happen to you!' (Matthew 16:22).

Perhaps the 'Barnabas and Saul' of your fellowship come back from a student missionary conference, a two-week mini-mission or a summer of service sensing the greatness of God's plan of the ages and their privileged part in it. Perhaps in your church, as in too many others, few barely rouse themselves to hear these enthusiasts report on what God is doing globally. As the church nods off, the potential missionaries say, 'Could you not listen for just one minute to what I believe God has in store for us?'

The cross-cultural worker goes back to the Rock and prays again, 'Father, there must be some other way for you to accomplish your purpose than by having me go.'

'No, my child. This is the way. Walk in it.' And his hour comes. No support is given. All scatter. The cross-cultural worker faces the Judases and priests and mobs of this world alone—unless you are there to give your moral support.

Worries about public opinion can hurt a missionary. Perhaps the potential cross-cultural worker is told, 'Okay, if you must go, go. But don't rock the boat. Don't get people here involved—especially financially. What will happen to our other projects?'

Fortunately, it is getting harder and harder for churches to have this attitude because missionary societies and those agencies helping to prepare cross-cultural workers for service are insisting that the local fellowship take the initiative in the missions process.

However, tragically, there are still thousands of cases in which a mission candidate's pastor is the 'last to know.' Or perhaps he never finds out! Public opinion in some churches does not allow for radical moves into international evangelization. So the cross-cultural worker has to leave very quietly—unless you are there to shout an encouraging, 'Bon voyage!'

Other attitudes dry up your cross-cultural worker's supply of moral support.

Competition within the body of Christ scares some fellowships into undermining a mission candidate's moral support. The message might be very strong: 'We don't want to lose you.'

The problem was not that the Jews did not believe in world evangelization. For Christ said of them, 'You travel over land and sea to win a single convert' (Matt. 23:15). Nor was it that they were against his healing people. But throngs of people were following Jesus. He was a threat to the establishment. He was the competition. He didn't fit into their programmes.

The bold, the daring, the assertive plans of the world missionary community don't fit into the programmes of a lot of today's churches, either—unless you are there to encourage Christ's example of unity in diversity.

Even the concern of friends can discourage a missionary when expressed in contradictory advice. The apostle Paul sensed at every turn the potential of the enemy's move. 'I will stay on at Ephesus until Pentecost, because a great door for effective work has opened to me and there are many who oppose me' (1 Cor. 16:8,9). At Miletus he said, 'Compelled by the Spirit, I am going to Jerusalem, not knowing what will happen to me there. I only know that in every city the Holy Spirit warns me that prison and hardships are facing me' (Acts 20:22, 23).

Days later, in Tyre, the disciples told Paul, through the Spirit, not to go to Jerusalem, But Paul and his friends continued their journey as far as Caesarea. There, in the house of Philip, Agabus took Paul's belt, tied his own hands and feet with it and warned: 'The Holy Spirit says, "In this way the Jews of Jerusalem will bind the owner of this belt. . . ." ' Luke recalls how 'when we heard this, we and the people there pleaded with Paul not to go up to Jerusalem.' So, instead of receiving support, Paul had to face discouragement. Luke remembered his response: 'Why are you weeping and breaking my heart? I am ready not only to be bound, but also to die in Jerusalem for the name of the Lord Jesus.' So, says Luke, 'when he would not be dissuaded, we gave up and said, "The Lord's will be done" ' (Acts 21:10–14).

The one who is boldly doing the work of the Lord is left alone—unless you are there to provide moral support to sustain your missionary in his difficult times when the adversaries are opposing him.

Distorted theological views can end up damaging the morale of a cross-cultural worker. The missionary heart of God is pierced again and again as fellowships deny the biblical injunctions to go, preach, and teach.

Some shout it as brashly as did William Carey's contemporaries: 'God will do it without us if he wants it done!' Others say it more subtly: 'We're too young as a fellowship. We're not big enough yet. No one in our fellowship seems interested. We don't have the resources to support a missionary. I don't have the time to devote to another new project. We would only want to send our best, and we can't afford to lose our leadership.'

Those excuses and a thousand more have all been thought or spoken. Yet not one of them stands the test of exposure to Scripture. Each excuse shrinks into the shadows, trying to hide from the light of his Word. There is

no theology to deny the missionary heartbeat of our God
who is 'not wanting anyone to perish, but everyone to come
to repentance' (2 Pet. 3:9).

Therefore, the cross-cultural parts of the body—and
there are cross-cultural parts, or else it is not a body—hang
lifeless in atrophy for lack of exercise. Or if they are challenged by another church or agency, their home church is
jealous because they are drawn away. And we are all the
losers for it.

The story is told of a young sailor who was making final
preparations for a solo voyage around the world in his
homemade craft. Throngs of people crowded the small
mooring as he stowed away the last boxes of provisions. A
murmuring air of pessimistic concern exploded into a
volume of discouragement: 'Son, you'll never make it!
That boat will not withstand the waves of the storms!
You'll run out of food! The sun will fry you!'

A late arrival, hearing all these discouraging warnings,
felt an irresistible desire to offer some optimism and encouragement. As the little craft began sailing away from
the pier, he pushed his way to the end of the dock. Waving
his hands wildly, he kept shouting, *'Bon voyage!* You're
really somebody! We're with you! We're proud of you!
God be with you, brother!'

The world seems to offer two kinds of support: 'Wait till
you get out in that cold, cruel world. It's rough!' And those
who exude a contagious, confident *'Bon voyage!'*

There are dozens of thoughtless ways to burst the balloon
of your aspiring missionary. But there are also plenty of ways
you can buoy up her enthusiasm with solid moral support.

Some Holy Spirit-guided soul-searching of our own
attitudes toward cross-cultural ministry would be good at
this point. An initial clearing of these 'stones of
incrimination' will make way for another type of

stone—the foundation for building a strong support system for the cross-cultural outreach ministry of your church.

How to Give Solid-As-a-Rock Moral Support

Dan had heard the call of God to go. He had visited Thailand on several occasions. There he had seen the hunger of pastors to learn to study the Word. He had experienced the joy of helping them satisfy that hunger through the seminars he taught.

And now Dan was sure God was directing him to a longer-term commitment: to establish a ministry conducting seminars for national pastors of Asia, seminars designed to train pastors in the study of the Word of God, thus allowing them better to feed their flocks.

But Dan was the pastor of a church in the United States. It would not be easy to leave. He had founded the church. Who would fill his position? How could he uproot his family and move them into the unknown? What about the finances and logistics of that move? What about communication and prayer? Where would they live when they came home?

All of these questions and apprehensions were real and needed answers. But they were more easily handled because the entire congregation gave their full moral support to what they sensed from the Lord to be a 'new thing' for Dan and for them!

Moral support is the foundation of the sending process. Moral support is the 'Bon voyage' of those who serve as senders to those who go. Moral support is as much an attitude that your cross-cultural worker will sense as an action you can perform.

Let's look at some solid foundation stones.

Jesus is the Chief Cornerstone

First, of course there has to be a cornerstone, '. . . a tried stone, a precious cornerstone, for a sure foundation' (Isaiah 28:16). In Jesus' day, the cornerstone was not some memorial plaque set into the wall after the building was completed. It was the first stone laid. All measurements of height, length and breadth were taken from it. If it were well-placed, the building had a good chance of being well-constructed. But if it were poorly laid, watch out!

Christ's life and teachings were an example of moral support. In fact, when Matthew wrote his gospel, the Holy Spirit inspired him to recall how Jesus fulfilled Isaiah's prophecy. 'A bruised reed he will not break, and a smouldering wick he will not snuff out' (Matthew 12:20 quoting Isaiah 42:3). A more modern rendering is, 'He does not crush the weak, nor snuff out the smallest candle flame'. 'He doesn't kick you when you're down!' might be an appropriate paraphrase.

What *does* he do?

He takes the bruised reed by the hand and, lifting her up, says, 'Where are they? Has no one condemned you? Then neither do I condemn you. Go now and leave your life of sin.' (John 8:10,11). He meets the 'smoking flax' at night since Nicodemus feared the Jews; he gently breathes the Spirit of life into the failing embers (John 3:1–21). Simon Peter's tears of remorse had all but extinguished his flame of fire. Jesus tenderly fans those failing embers back to life with his trilogy of poignant questions: 'Simon, do you love me? Feed my sheep!' (John 21:15–18).

His example of refusing to condemn and determining to encourage is the cornerstone of our support structure as we serve as senders. But it's not enough just to do his deeds. No amount of human-level determination will

equip you to be an adequate sender if you're not an inti-
mate disciple of Jesus Christ. This topic is beyond our focus
of study, but every sender, every sending team must be
personally, constantly communing with the One who in
moral support told us, 'As the Father has sent me, I am
sending you' (John 20:21).

The Simplicity of Moral Support

The cornerstone has been laid. We can begin building. The
first foundation stone that nudges right up and fits so
perfectly beside the chief cornerstone is the moral support
of the church that helps cross- cultural workers to 'Do it
simply—and simply do it!'

Jesus was a master at reducing to simplicity the impas-
sioned issues of his day—and ours.

On the complex issue of taxation, he said, 'Whose image
is on the coin?'

'Caesar's,' was the answer.

'Well, you had better give it to him then. But also give
to God what belongs to him!'

We spend hours questioning what life is all about.
Where did we come from? Jesus simply said, 'I came from
the Father.' We spend days wondering why we're here.
Jesus said, 'I am doing the will of the Father.' We spend
years worrying where we're going. Jesus said, 'I am going
to the Father.' In simple yet precise terms, he answered the
three universal questions of life! (See John 13:1–15.)

Jesus' ministry was deep, yet simple. And his lifestyle
was also simple. He was born in a stable. He had no place
to call home. His body occupied a borrowed tomb at his
death.

As your cross-cultural workers begin taking their steps
toward the fields of the world, they will be bombarded by

a thousand opportunities and ways to minister. Encourage them to keep their eyes focused on the simple, straightforward ministry of Jesus. Urge them to listen quietly to the direction of the Spirit out of all the godly counsel they are receiving. (See Prov. 19:20–21.) Remind them to keep it simple; your worker is not some new messiah! Advise them also simply to do it—to keep going one step at a time.

Help him or her practise a 'wartime lifestyle' even before going abroad. This doesn't mean living under an austere, ascetic vow of poverty. It means trimming off what isn't necessary. It means not spending on some things and spending strategically on others—much as a soldier going into combat doesn't need a gold-embossed jogging suit but does need a very expensive, state-of-the-art rifle.

Encouraging simplicity in ministry goals and in lifestyle is moral support!

Integrating Missions

The next foundation stone also fits snugly in its place. Support your worker in their understanding that mission is an *integrated* ministry of the church. Cross-cultural outreach is not the only God- ordained ministry.

'Yes, it is exciting to see that God has chosen you to minister cross-culturally. Yes, the zeal of the Lord is upon you,' you can agree with your missionary friend. But then you must remind him that the Sunday school teachers who tolerated his junior school age distractions are now dealing with the next generation of potential missionaries. Therefore, their work continues to be vital.

All the parts of the body work together in one direction within the 'unchangeable purpose of God' (see Hebrews 6:11–18), each adding its own expertise. Some of these ministries relate directly to that ultimate purpose of the church—to bless with the good news every people, tribe and tongue. And some are indirectly related.

You can encourage your missionary to remember that an accurate, big-picture world-view integrates ministries; it doesn't eliminate some nor value one ministry above another.

God's great purpose incorporates every God-given discipline in your life, every ministry in the life of your church. For example:

When your church members visit the elderly they can mention specific prayer requests of the urgent needs of all the ministries of the church. They can teach the elderly how to pray against the strongholds of Satan over a particular people group your missionary is targeting. They can infuse into each housebound person's remaining days a sense of purpose—'You can spend time in prayer that we can't! You know more about life than we do; therefore you can pray specifically for the ups and downs of our mission team. You can help open the way for the gospel in this group as you pray against the principalities and powers that rule and blind them! We need you!' A church ministry to housebound individuals can be incorporated into the vision of Christ's global cause, whether they pray for your missionary or for the church's prison ministry.

Every God-ordained ministry of the church can be expanded as it aligns its purposes with the great, unchangeable purpose of God. The life of the whole body—not just the cross-cultural parts—must remain strong. Therefore, the worship leaders must continue to usher us into the very throne room of God, and the Bible teachers must continue to feed the flock. And the other outreach ministries of the church must continue to reach out.

This is not easy for a missionary to appreciate as they get into their ministry. Their part of the big picture of God's purpose can easily become the only activity they see. Therefore, you enter as their moral supporter to give them a godly perspective.

You are able to help them recognize that moral support is a two-way street: To enjoy the moral support of others demands that one be interested in and an encouragement to them in their endeavours.

Active Listening

Another foundation stone of moral support is the art of active listening. Paul Tournier in his book *To Understand Each Other* said, 'Most conversations of this world are "dialogues of the deaf." ' Emotional isolation is already a major problem in Anglo-Saxon cultures. So when your friend is grappling with all the uncertainties of moving into cross-cultural outreach ministry, he needs even greater support: he needs your listening ear.

When your friend shares her thoughts about cross-cultural involvement, your ministry of moral support is most effective as you simply sit and listen.

Active listening is probably one of the most neglected foundation stones of moral support. *Active listening* says, 'I am with you. I will take the time. I will put energy into really listening to your heart, not just to what your surface words are saying.'

Active listening calls for all your attention. It is hard work; it requires concentration. But how necessary it is to moral support!

Active listening demands that you respond with respect. Even though you are not 'in his shoes' and cannot fully comprehend what he is experiencing, you can express empathy. Try to sense his thoughts and feelings as he anticipates his venture of faith.

Active listening demands feedback. Repeat in your own words what you heard being said. This will enable the speaker to assess whether or not you have heard right, and will give assurance of your support. He may then feel able to talk through problems with you, perhaps finding some solutions. Your active listening and repeating what you thought you heard will result in a great show of solid moral support!

Just being there to listen with positive feedback helps your missionary clarify their thoughts and feelings on a host of new concepts they must process.

We all know the risks of international travel. We all know the dangers of terrorist activity. We all know the socio-political issues related to the rise in nationalism. We all know the fears of the unknown. God does, too. Yet he says go!

Will you be one of those who will say, 'Wow! What a privilege to be about our Father's business!'? Will you offer, 'We're with you! What can we do to help?' You can be one who shouts, 'God bless you! We're proud of you! You're really something! *Bon voyage!*'

Stone by stone, the foundation of moral support is being laid.

Commissioning as Moral Support

There may be other stones of solid moral support that his Spirit will bring to your mind. But for now let's consider just three more stones that are vital to this foundation: called, counselled and commissioned. The church in Antioch provides a model from which we can draw our examples.

They put five men forward: they fasted and prayed.
They heard the Holy Spirit say, 'We want Barnabas and
Saul.' They fasted and prayed some more; they laid their
hands on them. They sent them away. Who is 'they'? The
church, the local body of believers—those who were sharing their own concern for this ministry that was burning
deep in the hearts of Barnabas and Saul (see Acts 13).

Called.
The church, the home group, the missions fellowship, the
prayer group, the college and career class—some group
besides the ones wanting to go needs to hear the Holy Spirit
say, 'Set apart for me (the Barnabas and Saul from your
fellowship) for the work to which I have called them' (Acts
13:2). This confirmation provides tremendous moral support! It is one thing for your missionaries to think the Lord
has directed them. It is incredibly more reassuring to know
he has confirmed it in the hearts of others as well.

Counselled.
The church fasted and prayed some more (Acts 13:3).
Though Scripture isn't specific as to their prayers, it's
apparent they were seeking guidance from the Lord for
details of this new venture. The passage implies that a
group larger than the two going heard answers to these
questions: How should they go? Where is the money coming from? What do they take with them? When should they
go? What are they going to do when they get there? Where
is *there*? (See Matthew 10:1–16.)
    This was a first as this team of senders determined how
they could best be supportive to some of the church's first
missionaries. Remember, the Antioch church was filled
with ordinary human beings. Yet they were able to carry

the weight of these unprecedented decisions as a team of people who had, in fasting and prayer, heard the Lord's direction.

Commissioned.

The senders laid their hands on the missionaries (Acts 13:3).

In Hebrews 6, the laying on of hands is named as one of the foundational doctrines. In this situation, the event was a commissioning, a setting-apart for a specific task, an identifying with the new ministry of the sent ones.

Whether your cross-cultural worker is going short-term or longer, they need the spiritual covering—the moral support—of 'the laying on of hands,' because, as an extension of your church's ministry, they are going out to battle against the enemy.

Identifying with your missionary, of course, means that you'll need to do some fine-tuning of your understanding of what they'll be facing. You need to know what God is doing these days in cross-cultural outreach ministry. Become an expert on the steady progress of the 21st century's Great Commission endeavour.

Read how Jackie Pullinger broke through the Walled City of Hong Kong in *Chasing the Dragon*. Marvel at how a 19-year-old touched the lives of Latin American Indians in *Bruchko* by Bruce Olson. Weep in sorrow at the price Christ paid for the lost of Russia as you read *Vanya* by Myrna Grant or *Tortured For His Faith* by Haralan Popov. Understand the cost of commitment in Pakistani Muslim Bilquis Sheikh's *I Dared to Call Him Father*. *Anointed for Burial* recounts God's work in Cambodia just before its fall. F. Kefa Sempangi gives a first person account of the martyrdom of Christians in Uganda in *A Distant Grief*. Rejoice that God has placed *Eternity in Their Hearts* as examined in Don Richardson's book on redemptive analogy, a key to proclaiming Christ to the nations. (See 'Resources', beginning on page 201 for information on obtaining these and other cutting-edge materials on today's mission to the world.)

As you identify with your missionary's work, what you learn about God's work around the world will bring a deeper sense of your part in God's global purpose and of how your role is critical as you give moral support to those who say, 'I believe the Lord wants me to go to the mission field! And I want you, church, to send me!'

A Case Study in Moral Support

More members of the sending team we met in Chapter One recount some of their experiences in learning how to offer their missionaries some solid moral support:

> Those of us who know Lou and Sandy personally would probably sum up our offers of moral support to them in these words: 'We love you and are here to help you in any way we can. We believe in the vision the Lord has given you to go to the Philippines. But in our eagerness to help you on your way, don't lose sight of the fact that we will greatly miss you.'
>
> After the core group—which is what we call the leadership of our Lou-and-Sandy support team—was established in June, things began to roll at seemingly breakneck speed. Looking back on it all now, we see that the moral support we gave was intertwined with our actions in all the other areas of support. When Lou and Sandy had to get out of their house and into temporary lodgings for a month before leaving for training in Mexico, a home was graciously opened to them.
>
> Have you ever prepared for a garage sale? Lou and Sandy had to go through everything they owned: Do we sell this? Store it? Take it with us? Ultimately the decisions were Lou's

and Sandy's, but to be nearby with a listening ear and an opinion was part of our moral support. The willingness of people to find boxes, store things safely, build a crate for shipment, advertise the sale, price everything and bring meals again and again after the pots and pans were packed expressed the moral support so needed and appreciated by Lou and Sandy.

Since they have left, we have found other ways to give moral support. On their last Sunday at church we had a large banner made which said, '*Bon voyage*, Lou, Sandy and Marlies.' We later laid it out over several long tables and provided pens for people to write some words of encouragement. We sent the banner by boat so they would receive it after having been there for several months.

The enthusiasm and excitement that still accompanies any of the activities we arrange for our missionaries lets us know the moral support is running high. Though letter writing generally falls into the category of communication support, the fact that Lou and Sandy receive so many letters is most certainly a boost to their morale. In one six-week period, they reported they had gone only three days without receiving at least one letter, and one day they had received seven!

Moral support is obviously basic if you're serving as a sender. Maybe your forte as a sender will be boosting your missionary's morale.

But other areas of support are important, too, if your sent-one is going to be fully supported. Somebody has to help with the nuts and bolts of stretching your fellowship's ministry from Jerusalem to Judea to Samaria and to the uttermost parts of the earth! Missionaries need careful, solid *logistics* support.

(In addition to the individual study below, see the **Group Leader's Guide** for session two beginning on page 201.)

For Your Personal Involvement

- Read Matthew 12:20 from a number of translations. Choose one that really communicates the message to you. Memorize it. Meditate on it. Allow the Holy Spirit to infuse this concept of moral support deep into your being.
- Read, in its context, the story of each of the individuals in the Bible we referred to. Place next to their names the relationship of the people who could have been of moral support to them:

David, 1 Samuel 30 _____
Jesus, Luke 22 _____
Mary, Matthew 1 _____
The blind man, John 9 _____
Paul, Acts 21 _____

- Choose one of the stories. In your own words, retell the story as if those people *had* given moral support.
- Think of some advertising slogans that, if followed, could easily distract you from giving moral support to your missionaries. For example: 'When the going gets tough, the tough go shopping.'

What are some *biblical* sayings to govern our actions in moral support? (For example, Galatians 6:2.)

Action Steps

By the time you have read Chapter Two, completed the *For Your Personal Involvement* section and participated in a discussion group, you should . . .

- Understand that moral support is the basic foundation of the support system.
- Be ready to express appreciation and give moral support to everyone in the fellowship who is a functioning part of the body.
- Realize that moral support is an ongoing relationship with your missionary.
- Write to one of your missionaries on the field and say, 'Here is my belated *"Bon voyage!"* God bless you!'
- Involve others. You might be surprised how contagious enthusiastic moral support becomes! Encourage others with the practice of encouragement!

Chapter Three

Logistics Support

'When you come, bring the cloak that I left with Carpus at Troas and my scrolls, especially the parchments.'

2 Timothy 4: 13

'Sure, I had had some good training in building a support team. I had made provision for my logistics support. A very nice fellow named Bill had said he would handle everything. Looking back, that should have been my first clue that it might not work out. *Nobody* can handle everything! But I didn't think of it at the time.

'A ministry opportunity had opened up. We had been invited to lead some relief work in the Middle East. We sensed God's direction in this. Things were coming together well. A lot of clothes and medicine were being given to us to distribute once we got there. We neatly packed and identified each box. Bill said that when sailors from our church came to a nearby military installation, he would get each of them to bring a few. Or he was sure he could arrange space for the whole shipment through diplomatic channels. What a relief to my mind. I could concentrate on other details.

'Three years later, we came home for a short visit. I sheepishly went to the friend who had let us store those boxes in his garage for these three years. Yep! They were all there! Just as we had left them! Not one had been sent to us.

'We shipped the stuff to a ministry in Mexico. They said they could use what wasn't outdated. I took the few remaining boxes of our personal items to Bill. "Yeah, sure! No problem. Those will be on the next ship out!"

'Well, we're ready to come home on furlough again. We've decided that since we've made it for six years over here without that stuff, we really don't need it. It will be interesting, though, when we get home, to look through the boxes to see what one day had seemed so important to us.

'Bill's a good man. But he just didn't seem to be able to get those boxes over to us!'

Logistics support deals with handling the nuts and bolts of your cross-cultural worker's continuing home country responsibilities.

Logistics support must be considered on two levels: 1) Those areas of business to be attended to by the church leadership or missionary society and 2) the multitude of details that can be handled by a team of individuals. You, as part of the Logistics Support Team, could find yourself involved in:

- Identifying the cross-cultural workers in your fellowship.
- Maintaining accountability in ministry.
- Confirming and encouraging spiritual growth.
- Managing business affairs.
- Attending to personal details.

Identifying Cross-Cultural Workers

The local congregation, the body of Christ in microcosm, in order to function as a body, must have all the necessary parts. The body needs a mouth, so he appointed some prophets and pastor/teachers. The body needs to function 'decently and in order,' so he gave some the gift of administration.

He even has someone always 'just hanging around' like the appendix! And because *outreach* is one of the main functions of the Church, and because he said, 'The field is the world' (Matthew 13:38), God has placed in every body parts that are to minister cross-culturally.

In many churches, cross-cultural workers have not been given the opportunity to exercise their gifts, so they sit in atrophy, wondering, 'Why am I here?' They may try to find a place of ministry in some other area, but they just don't fit in! So in frustration they move from one ministry to another—or from one church to another.

The first logistical responsibility of the church, then, is to provide for the identification and exercise of the cross-cultural parts.

When Barnabas and Saul returned to Antioch from Jerusalem with some firsthand reports from the apostles, the church identified and put forth five men—prophets and teachers, leaders in the church. Then, in prayer and fasting, *the church* heard the Holy Spirit say, 'I want Barnabas and Saul for some cross-cultural work' (A rather loose paraphrase of Acts 13: 1–2!)

The local fellowship of believers must take the initiative in the missionary process by identifying the cross-cultural parts of the body and allowing them to exercise their gifts.

A missions fellowship at your church, then, becomes an ideal testing ground for potential missionaries. Under the direction of a lay or staff leader, those who believe they are your body's cross- cultural parts can experience all aspects of missions. They can be challenged to the task of cross-cultural outreach ministry by speakers and cultural studies and reports. They can practise the art of missionary support—moral, logistics and so on. They can exercise their gifts by ministering to people from overseas in your own home town. As potential *goers* are identified, they can actually go on a mini-mission or short-term experience. And the identified *senders* can serve as their senders!

The pastor, missions committee or fellowship should not be the last to know when one of the members from your church is getting involved in missions! Take the initiative: make cross-cultural outreach a part of the vision God has given you for your fellowship.

Maintaining Accountability in Ministry

Accountability has become one of the catchwords of our culture. And wouldn't one expect a reaction—at some time—to the 'do your own thing' philosophy? Yet, there are pastors and church leaders who do not know what those who have gone out from their church are doing. Some say, 'Well, they're with XYZ Society. Isn't that a good mission?'

Quite possibly. But. . . .

Does that mission reflect the ministry goals of your church? Is that ministry targeting a decisive point of battle? Are your missionary's abilities and giftings suited to the work of that mission?

A second dimension of this responsibility then follows: Once you are sure your cross-cultural worker is involved in a ministry suited to their gifts and the ministry thrust of your church, you must have some ongoing evaluation to know if that ministry is progressing. A regular, independent report from their supervisor will keep you in touch with their work.

If your missionary is working through a missionary society, make sure the lines of accountability are open, defined and include your fellowship. Remember, this missionary is still a part of your body.

A report from your worker should fill in the details. A periodic phone call, an occasional report from another worker in the area—even a visit by an appointed elder from your church—would assure you that the ministry is really happening.

After all, the work of those who go and those who serve as senders is a team effort!

Confirming Spiritual Growth

Sadly, some sets of statistics report that for all their preparation, for all their 'hearing God's voice' and for all their support, up to 50% of cross-cultural workers do not complete their *first* term of service.

Too many of them don't make it because of spiritual drought. They have dried up spiritually. They have come to the point where they are trying to give out more than they are taking in.

Church leadership must encourage spiritual growth 1) before missionaries go, 2) while they're on the field, and 3) when they return home.

1)   Encouragement in spiritual growth before they go.
Antioch provides a good example: Barnabas and Saul were mature leaders chosen by the Holy Spirit for a very tough assignment. It is easy to study their fine qualifications in Scripture.

For some reason, however, they took John Mark along. Evidently he was not prepared; when the going got tough, he quit!

Several years later, Paul sensed that John Mark *still* was not ready (Acts 15:38). But then several years after that assessment, Paul told Timothy to bring Mark with him, for 'he is helpful to me in my ministry' (2 Timothy 4:11).

A goer's eagerness to be sent doesn't necessarily mean he or she is *ready* to be sent.

One church does it this way: All those who even think they are cross-cultural parts of the body are encouraged to attend the missions fellowship headed by a cross-cultural coordinator. Here they are regularly exposed to cross-cultural outreach through prayer for the peoples of the world, speakers and videos of ministries and opportunities for ministry, including short-term awareness and ministry trips.

As a person (or couple) *and* the group sense the call of the potential goer, that person begins relating with the senior pastor in personal discipleship training. After functioning for a time in some position of leadership, the person is ready for cultural training and developing a personal support team.

The church must send a capable, credible worker—one who knows what they believe and why. That confidence may come through in-house training, being sent to a Bible school or a combination of several preparation programmes.

The church must send those who have stripped the gospel and teachings of Christ of all European, American and Hebrew culture so that they can allow the host culture to clothe the gospel in garb suitable to it.

Senders must send one who has been trained in interpersonal relationships, the lack of which is the greatest reason for missionary dropouts! The church must not send one who is 'always learning but never able to acknowledge the truth' (2 Tim 3:7), but one who is 'growing in the knowledge of God' (Colossians 1:10).

2) Encouragement in spiritual growth on the field.

Once a field worker becomes unencumbered with the affairs of his life at home (see 2 Timothy 2:4) and is thrust into the midst of endless opportunities for ministry, it is *very easy* for them to neglect their own spiritual intake—to be working so hard for the Vine that the branch becomes pinched and the life- sustaining sap is cut off.

Soon yesterday's prayers, last week's Bible reading, last month's study of the word of God are not able to sustain the worker through today's demands and he or she falls prey to spiritual drought.

The writer of Hebrews says, 'By this time you ought to be teachers but you need someone to teach you. . . . Let's not (lay) again the foundation . . . (but) go on to maturity' (Hebrews 5:12–6:3).

Not having Christian radio and TV stations and several Bible studies to choose from each week, your worker must be a student of the Bible—one who correctly handles the word of truth, a workman who does not need to be ashamed (2 Timothy 2:15). They must know how to feed themselves spiritually.

You may help in this area perhaps by sending Bible study tapes, or by getting them to enrol on to a correspondence course. Perhaps you can study together by letter on a book by book Bible study.

One missionary family in Peru arranged for their church to send weekly Bible study tapes. They soon began to listen to them in a group Bible study with other team members. Before long many groups were organized and listening! When they heard a few new choruses on the study tapes, they began to miss their Christian music. They quickly got on the ham radio to ask a support team member to send some Christian music tapes—soon!

3) *Encouragement in spiritual growth when they come back home.*

Your missionary may come home for a brief stay before returning to the field. Check their spiritual temperature. Many have been bombarded by new ideas and ideals, different values and beliefs. Are the changes in their thinking only cultural? Or has a subtle pantheism or another deceptive outlook permeated their doctrine? He or she may need their faith strengthening, or, more seriously, a redefining of their Christian foundations. Some slightly askew winds of doctrine may even have come from the isolated team of the organization through which they are working.

If your worker has come home to take up a new ministry here, you cannot assume that spiritual growth will continue. Here at home one is bombarded by the gods of materialism and hedonism. These can have a drastic effect on doctrine! Make sure he is still sharing what he 'received' (1 Corinthians 15:3).

A certain family served on a two-year mission assignment in the Far East. They returned home to resume ministry. It wasn't until much later—fifteen years later—through the counsel of their church leadership, that they came to understand the intensity of the spiritual assault that had been launched against their whole family while overseas. They then began to work on breaking the powers of darkness and the resulting destructive patterns and began to live in the victorious freedom available in Christ. Supportive, intense prayer for them by the church when they first came home might have identified this problem sooner.

Managing Business Affairs

If your worker goes through a missionary society, most of the following issues will be established by the society's policy. Reading through some of these perplexing logistics might make you appreciate what a society goes through to keep missionaries overseas. Even if these tasks are handled by a society it is still your responsibility to know its policies and how you as the sending church relate to them. More and more missionary societies are asking for the church to be more actively involved in the whole missions process—including logistics.

If your church sends out missionaries directly to work with national ministries or to plant churches in unreached groups, think through each of the following issues first and plan carefully. And remember that the list is only a cursory look at the business matters that will come up!

1) Money
This conjures up more emotion than any other in the whole arena of missions! Because of its importance, someone in the church leadership must be responsible for handling the details.

a) Work with the national ministry and your cross-cultural worker to determine a necessary and adequate monthly budget.

b) Establish acceptable methods for securing enough financial support.

c) Record and communicate how each donor identifies their gift as designated for a particular missionary and/or project.

d) Develop a system for receipting the donor and for notifying your cross-cultural worker of amounts and who donated. Careful financial monitoring is needed to transfer those funds overseas. Will any be kept back for administering the funding process? What will you do if donations fall below the established quota?

2) Taxes

How easily Jesus reduced to simplicity the whole issue of taxes (see Matthew 33:15–22). But earthly governments seem to be able to make things very complicated. Therefore 'rendering unto Caesar' requires an astute mind aware of the myriads of details involved. Details such as deductions, tax status changes caused by your worker's being 'non- gainfully employed', length of residence outside the UK, the host country's tax system etc. are just the tip of the iceberg. If your fellowship does not have the time to keep up with all the laws, find a tax professional who can help with your missionary's situation *before* you send your worker to the field—just to make sure all is in order in this vital area of logistics support.

Don't let your cross-cultural worker become a horror story of trouble with the Inland Revenue.

3) Health

Responsible church leaders will make sure their cross-cultural worker and the whole family are in good health—physically, emotionally, mentally and spiritually before they go to the field. Leaders must further see that their health care needs overseas are met in an appropriate way.

Definitely related to the health and well-being of your cross-cultural worker is their safety. What will you as a sending church do if your worker gets into trouble in the host culture? What if he or she is caught in the cross-fire of

a civil disturbance? What if the government is over-
thrown? What if your worker is kidnapped?

The list goes on. Some hard facts! But it is far better to
have these issues thought out ahead of time and to have a
plan of action in place than to wait until your worker's
phone call from prison to begin thinking about such
matters!

4) Death

Death is an inevitable fact of life. Yet this most emotionally
charged event is sometimes totally unplanned for by a
missionary's sending church. To clarify the necessary details, your fellowship must plan ahead.

It is generally accepted that the best place to be buried
is where one dies. Many countries do not embalm; therefore they require burial within 24 hours.

The cost of immediate or even chartered flights out of a
country is usually prohibitive. Furthermore, 'N lived,
worked, died and is buried among us,' is a powerful statement of the incarnation of Christ in your cross-cultural
worker among a targeted people group. Their testimony
lives on!

A further emotionally charged consideration is the expense of a missionary coming home for the funeral of a
relative. Do you tell your missionary that you simply can't
afford to fly him or her home to comfort their mother at
father's funeral because you weren't prepared? Will you
take up a special offering for such an emergency? Do you
maintain an emergency fund?

Carefully think through these and other life-and-death
policies.

Attending to Personal Details

Beyond this array of details that are best handled by the missionary society and church leaders under their spiritual and corporate covering, there is a host of bits and pieces of logistical matters that can be handled by an individual. The list here merely suggests a few of the innumerable situations that could arise with your particular field worker.

1) Material goods

If their car didn't sell before they left, you could hold power of attorney to sell it for them—at agreed terms, of course. You could manage the rental or lease of their house. You could make payments from their bank account for property, insurance or other financial commitments. You could send them the proper income tax forms, licence-renewal forms, credentials or certificates. You could store the boxes of personal belongings which they chose not to sell or take with them. And, of course, you could arrange to send necessary materials to them on time!

2) Family matters

You may be called upon to be executor of your missionary's will. You may be asked to serve as the guardians of their children if death should occur. You may be the ideal person to visit or care for their elderly parents. You may be able to provide a home for a student son or daughter attending college in your town. You may have the contacts to provide the home–schooling curriculum materials they need. You may represent your missionary at family gatherings or events.

3) Ministry needs

You could collect and post ministry items to your workers—Bibles, food and clothing for the poor, Sunday school
materials and pictures. Since prices of many types of tech-
nical equipment are much lower in the UK you could
become your missionary's source for information and purchase of computers, modem, fax machines or hand-crank
or solar-powered cassette players. You could possibly help
also with the supply of blank audio/video tapes.

These jobs only suggest the size and diversity of this
important support role. Selected members of your sending
team with real gifts of service must attend to all your
worker's responsibilities that continue in the home country.

Logistics support is essentially caring for each other in
the body of Christ. The Bible teaches a simple doctrine: We
really do need each other. We are the family of God, the
body of Christ. Paul simply said that the body should work
together as a whole with all the members having the same
care one for another (1 Corinthians 12:25).

Logistics support members must have certain qualifications:

Diligence: Sometimes it takes a bit of research to find all
the correct income tax forms. Sometimes it takes some
creative looking to find an inexpensive source (or any
source) for New Testaments in the Uzbek language!

Concern for detail: Using the post effectively— complet-
ing the customs forms, packaging, postage, labelling—
takes time and communication with the field worker
regarding postal requirements in the host country and
detailed concern in working with the Royal Mail or other
carrier. In the UK, the Royal Mail produces a series of

leaflets about how to send parcels etc. abroad, listing des-
tinations and charges. Many items can be sent in a 'jiffy
bag' or at 'small packet' rate. Customs forms and airmail
stickers are available at all post offices.

New missionaries in Peru got a notice from the Lima
post office that a parcel of homemade cookies had arrived.
When an exorbitant import duty was demanded for the
shipment, the missionaries decided they should pay it for
the sake of their relationship with the well-meaning senders . . . until an experienced missionary told them the parcel
would have been 'accidentally' damaged and all the cookies would be gone anyway! Logistics support must be
concerned with details such as import duties on parcels.

Punctuality: When you get a request for an item from
your cross-cultural worker, the chances are that a week or
two has already passed since the need became acute. Finding what was requested, packing and sending it—in addition to the return mail time—can cause quite a delay. Any
procrastination increases the wait.

Sound business practices: Your record-keeping and
promptness of payment in your missionary's financial
dealings is a reflection of *their* integrity in business.

One missionary family turned the management of the
rental of their house over to a friend. Bills and receipts
accompanied every cheque that this friend wrote. The
records were kept with accuracy. The businesslike manner
of their friend gave them confidence that all would be well
when they returned.

Be assured that the peace of mind you as a good logistics
support person can provide for a cross- cultural worker is
equal in value to the things you do for them. What a
privileged opportunity to serve as a sender!

Case Study in Logistics Support

The core group we have been following shows us more about this area of support:

The logistics support we provide for Lou and Sandy includes legal aspects such as serving as executors and keepers of their wills. It also involves taking care of some of their financial affairs such as income tax and life insurance payments. It has even included selling their car.

Lou and I were room-mates in college and have managed to remain close friends ever since. It was this long-standing relationship that led Lou to ask me to take care of his business while he and Sandy were in the Philippines. It seemed like a simple task: send occasional cheque, file a form or two . . . It was—I thought—no big deal!

As Lou and Sandy prepared to go to a training course in Mexico, they were very busy and we never seemed to find the time to get together. We finally found one half-hour to discuss how they ran their lives, what bills they had due each month and how we were going to handle their financial affairs. Additionally, we met at their bank to make me a signatory on their savings account and to complete a power of attorney form that authorized me to have full control of their business affairs.

As I started paying their bills, I quickly realized that I needed a system to keep records of what I had paid. Thankfully my wife is much more organized than I and produced an old bill-organizer that is working fine. It will hopefully provide them with a full account of what we have done when they return from the Philippines.

Taking over their financial affairs hasn't been easy. There have been those unexplained bills—like the demand from a life insurance company. Do I pay this? I didn't know how to handle this one!

Then there was the car! 'The Bomb,' as Lou affectionately called it, was one of those things that gives used car salesmen such a bad reputation. Suddenly I found myself faced with having to sell a car I wouldn't wish on my worst enemy! Fortunately, a mechanic friend of Lou's was willing to take it as a 'project' car.

The hardest part of what we are doing is the realization that we could really mess up someone else's business credibility, and that they are not in a position to do anything about it. It came to a head when we needed to find out if they wanted us to do their tax return or send all the information to them. As the April deadline approached, we realized that the post would not go back and forth fast enough to communicate.

We checked with the phone company and found the cheapest times to call that would still fit into both our schedules. After trying to connect for half an hour, we prayed that if the decision we had come to about their taxes was wrong, we would get through the next time. The next time, Lou answered the phone! We had made the wrong decision and were able to straighten out a number of nagging questions. Our peace of mind—and theirs as well—cost very little.

The lessons we logistics supporters have already learned about how to do this right include:

1) Sit down for several sessions with whoever you are sending. Even if they are going out with a well-known missionary society or association, don't assume that all their personal business matters will somehow be taken care of. Go over taxes, past and present. Discuss every financial obligation they have. Find out why they have these bills and why they pay them the way they do and whom to contact when questions arise.

2) Get a full power of attorney for a husband and wife separately.

3) Set up a record-keeping system before departure. Find out how they want their records maintained so that you don't just hand them a stack of old bills and cancelled cheques when they return.

4) Make sure that their wills are complete and on file with their executor. If that is you, get a safe deposit box. Make sure

they have expressed how they wish their remains to be disposed of. Lou, being a very practical guy said, 'The cheapest way possible!'

5) Pray about the responsibility you are about to accept. The enemy just loves to confuse and condemn anyone trying to do anything for the Lord—even something as simple (?) as paying a few bills!

This is logistics support at its best! There is no way of anticipating what your missionary will ask for; there is no knowing when a request will come. But one committed to the task and diligent in the work is a rare and prized partner in cross-cultural ministry. You may just be that person.

But for your missionary to sense the full support they need, other areas of your possible service become important also. In order that a missionary may become 'disentangled from the affairs of this life' and preach the Gospel freely, a vital part of the team becomes those who provide the *financial* support.

(In addition to the individual study below, see the **Group Leader's Guide** for session three beginning on page 182.)

For Your Personal Involvement

- Read Paul's account of co-operation in the Body of Christ from 1 Corinthians 12. Particularly note the care given to the "unpresentable" parts.
- In the Book of Acts, underline all references to travel logistics. With today's electronic communication systems, how could someone 'back home' have helped in each of these instances?
- Make a list of all the things in your life that would need attention 'back home' if you went away for two years.

These are probably the things your missionary will
need to find someone to handle.

Action Steps

By the time you have read Chapter Three, completed the
For Your Personal Involvement section and participated in a
group discussion, you should . . .

- Understand the potentially vast number of details involved in logistics support.
- Be more aware that we are the body of Christ and we
  really do need each other.
- Decide whether God wants you to be on the Logistics
  Support Team of a cross-cultural worker you know. If
  so, write to them and inquire about any logistical
  needs that they may have. Make yourself available to
  assist in that need.
- Involve others. As you come to understand the value
  of this type of support, encourage others to consider it
  as their place in the Body of Christ.

Chapter Four

Financial Support

'I rejoice greatly in the Lord that at last you have renewed your concern for me. Indeed, you have been concerned, but you had no opportunity to show it. I am not saying this because I am in need, for I have learned to be content whatever the circumstances. I know what it is to be in need, and I know what it is to have plenty. I have learned the secret of being content in any and every situation, whether well fed or hungry, whether living in plenty or in want.'

Philippians 4:10–12

'In totally miraculous ways God opened four major doors to bring us to Cameroon, West Africa, as Short-Term Assistants (STAs) with Wycliffe.

'Being STAs wasn't new to us. We had spent two eventful years in Mexico and later thought of serving again—some time. But I had no idea returning to the field was the reason for an appointment at 8 a.m. one September morning with Dan Harrison, Wycliffe's Superintendent of Children's Education.

'But the longer we talked, the more I wondered if God wanted us on the field again—now! By 9:30 we decided I wasn't the one to go to Nepal; by 10:30 I had some reservations about Papua New Guinea; by 11:00 a.m. we were praying for God's direction for me to be a principal-teacher in Cameroon.

' "We're going to Africa!" ' I announced as I walked through the front door of our home that day. While my wife Jill and I prayerfully considered the decision, we knew God would have to open several doors which could keep us from going if they remained closed.

'The first one was to do with our oldest son James, who was only a term away from graduation. Would it even be fair to him to change schools again? Though we definitely wanted him to go with us, it would have to be his decision. As days merged into weeks, his attitude changed from "Do your own thing, but don't expect me to go", to "Let's get going!"

'Our home represented another obstacle. How could we ever find a family to be totally responsible for the house for two years? But in God's time scale he brought close friends to Southern California for a furlough from their ministry with Wycliffe in Mexico. They moved in—we moved out, leaving pictures on the walls and sheets in the airing cupboard.

'A third problem was my mother-in-law's health. She was battling with cancer and really depending on Jill for moral support. God took care of her needs through a miraculous healing!

'The fourth door to be opened had dollar signs on it! We learned that the cost of living in Cameroon was as high as in Southern California. We sent a letter to our friends— those who we thought would be interested in what we felt sure God wanted us to do. Money began coming in. A bonus on the job. A buyer for the car and caravan. Our church had just decided to double its support for Wycliffe families. Friends pledged towards our monthly needs.

'We received official approval from the Wycliffe Board. Passports and immunizations were now in order. We were assured our visas would arrive between November 12th and 15th. We set our departure date: 10 p.m. November 18th from the Los Angeles airport.

'All the normal hectic things were happening: We were trying to buy lightweight clothing in winter; packing, weighing, repacking; finding a mislaid birth certificate; sending out another letter; having the last gala round of visits to friends.

'Then November 18th came. At 8 a.m. I was making the final check on our financial situation—a task I had intentionally delayed. I just couldn't make it all add up. We were $50 a month short.

' "I just cannot sign our Statement of Financial Preparedness," I regretfully told Jill. We all laughed at the ridiculousness of our situation. Luggage filled the living room. The kids had officially left school. Our car was sold. Our friends were already living with us—and wanted us to get out of their house! All goodbyes had been said. We were holding $3,000 worth of non-redeemable airline tickets in our hands. We'd radioed Africa that we were on our way. And here we were, $50 a month short of our support goal!

' "The Lord must be planning to send in some money today," I said as I put the statement aside, unsigned.

'At 9 a.m. Jill's mother called, asking if we needed any money. She then related an incredible story about Myrna, a lady in their church. She had been on our financial support team during our time with Wycliffe in Mexico. And she had heard us present the financial needs for this new venture in Cameroon. Unbeknown to us, she had been struggling for several weeks to find a way in which God could use her again on our financial support team.

'But it was now the night before we were to leave. Myrna spent a sleepless vigil asking the Lord for some way that she could still help us. Their business was in financial difficulties and their house had just been burgled. At 4 a.m.

she dozed off and at 7 a.m. was up preparing to go to a church missionary meeting. At 8 a.m. (while I was adding up) she put on a coat she hadn't worn since the previous winter. She put her hand in the pocket and, to her amazement, drew out $1,200 in cash! The thief who had so thoroughly gone through her husband's clothing in that wardrobe three nights before had completely missed her coat!

' "This is for the Coopers!" ' she shouted. 'Thank you, Lord for your faithfulness!'

'I said, "Praise the Lord" The $1,200 she found in the pocket and wanted us to have was exactly the $50 support for 24 months that we lacked. I ran for the Statement of Financial Preparedness and signed, "Yes, we are ready to go!" '

Financial support is the most controversial, thus the most talked-about of the six areas of support. In fact, when you mention missionary support, most people think of nothing else but money.

As Christians we must steer a course between two extremes. On the one hand, we are made to feel guilty by the millions who are starving to death because we do not give £5 to such-and-such an organization. At the other extreme, we are told 'Prosperity is your divine right!' Where do we turn for balance in financial responsibility?

To further complicate the issue is the problem that a god of this age in the West is materialism. The media create, then prey on, society's poor self-image by saying, 'You aren't good enough . . . until you use our product!' So we toil endlessly to purchase this and that, only to find out in the next commercial that a 'new and improved' version is now available. As the bumper sticker says, 'I owe, I owe, so off to work I go!' How do we rise above the trivia of this world to see financial responsibility from God's perspective?

His Word, of course, communicates his perspective. On the stub of every pay cheque received by Christians could be the words of Deuteronomy 8:18: 'Remember the Lord your God, for it is he who gives you the ability to produce wealth.' Why does God bless us with wealth?

God's principle that his people are blessed to be a blessing is established in the covenant he made with Abraham (see Genesis 12).

Some ways of raising money to bless the world through cross-cultural outreach ministry include cake sales and car washes, paper and can recycling. A garage sale with all or a portion of the proceeds going to a missions project or missionary can bring families together for good causes. Art and craft items can be made and sold and the profit given to a missionary. God blesses us with ingenuity, mouth-watering recipes and entrepreneurial skills so that financially we can bless the spread of his Kingdom.

But the time will come when all garages are clean, people will want to keep their remaining newspapers to light winter fires and everybody has had their fill of fundraising pizzas.

More likely, the time will come when your cross-cultural outreach ministry has grown beyond the funds that can be generated by these methods. And now diligent effort must be made to look beyond these efforts to more creative, long-lasting ways of raising money for cross-cultural outreach ministry. Let's look at three areas of biblical stewardship: giving, lifestyle and managing wealth.

Giving

We know the Bible says that God loves a cheerful giver. It is more blessed to give than to receive. Give, and it shall be given to you. When you give . . . Yet the brilliance of the Bible's simple teaching on the principle of giving invariably comes round to 'how much?' Which inevitably leads to tithing. Which ultimately deals with the nitty-gritty of, 'Do I tithe on my net or on my gross income?' And we have run into the same dead end as the Jews to whom Jesus said, 'You give a tenth of your spices—mint, dill and cummin. But you have neglected the more important matters of the law. . . . You strain out a gnat but swallow a camel.' (Mathew 23:23–24).

The discipline of tithing (which Jesus commended the Jews for practising) leads a Christian to a deeper commitment of 'cheerful' giving (2 Corinthians 9:7), which grows into the willing mind principle of 2 Corinthians 8:12–14: 'That there might be equality!'

Using this principle, as long as we compare ourselves only to those wealthier than we are, we don't feel too compelled to give. But when we enlarge our vision to encompass the world, the principle of equality has us giving and giving some more since the 'poverty' level in the West is equivalent to great wealth in most Third World countries. We are indeed rich.

A well-known hymn says: 'I surrender all, I surrender all. All to Jesus I surrender; I surrender all.' May we, in our responsible stewardship of finances, grapple with God's word and the work of the Holy Spirit in our lives to that point of full surrender.

Before we go on, let's look again at the basic concept. If every Christian in your fellowship tithed, that tithe would keep the finance committee busy meeting every week to decide on its disposal.

None of us likes to hear a 20-minute sermon on giving before each offering is taken. But the very concept of 'taking' an offering instead of 'Freely you have received, freely give' (Matthew 10:8) might be educating us to be miserly in our giving. Sometimes even the prayer said at offering time does more to support our meagre giving than to encourage a 'generous, cheerful, hilarious' freewill gift: 'Father, you know we only have these few pennies to give to you. But you multiply them so the whole world can believe in you!' And we put away our wallets and pull out our loose change—if we have any!

Or we are taught to 'pay' our tithes. As with any other bill, therefore, a conscious or unconscious resentment can develop. Rather, the Bible urges that God's people 'bring the whole tithe into the storehouse' (Malachi 3:10). 'Store up for yourselves treasure in heaven' (Matthew 6:20). That sounds more like securing a sound investment than 'paying a bill'. And that grows into, 'What a privilege to be part of God's plan of the ages. He could get along without my money, for he owns "the cattle on a thousand hills" ' (Psalm 50:10). But the Lord is giving me an opportunity to invest in his kingdom!

Giving is an act of intelligent worship. What do we learn from his word? That generous, cheerful, hilarious giving is not an awkward interruption to worship, but the very essence of it.

How can we be wise about our giving?

Unfortunately, not all individuals and organizations vying for your support are themselves wise stewards. There are three questions you must ask to check them on their accountability:

1) *Is the money you give going where they say?* Do they take 60 pence of your pound to raise additional funds? A dedicated sender once gave a very large donation to an international project. A year later, those who had solicited this gift came back to him, apologizing that they had not used the money as they had told him. Would he forgive them? Did he want his money back? An apology doesn't happen often! The funds are more likely to be hidden in the language of the bookkeeper's report!

2) *Is the project or missionary service really hitting a decisive point in the battle for souls?* God wants us to be a part of ministries that yield 'fruit that will last' (John 15:16).

You might even have to say 'no' to your closest friend's appeal if you sense his 'summer of service' sounds more like a surf and sun holiday!

Worthwhile missionary service is as diverse as the creative genius of God flowing through his obedient servants. And some of the activities seem way out there—somewhere! But if they are really hitting a decisive point in the battle for the souls of mankind, there will be a line of correlation that can be traced to 'fruit that will last.'

3) *If your cross-cultural worker is going out through a UK-based organization, what is the UK administrative/field use ratio of the mission's funds?* That is, how much is spent in the UK to get one pound to the field? Is it under 20%? Are the UK personnel living on a comparable level to their field workers? How do they raise money? (By the way, if an organization doesn't want to answer this type of question, you have a pretty good idea of its accountability already!)

Lifestyle

Statistics can bore or shock or motivate. For example: Americans spend as much on chewing gum in a year as they give to missions, and pay as much for pet food in 52 days as they spend annually on missions. Does our lifestyle, as Jesus said, tell us where our heart is?

The 'Queen Mary' was designed as a luxury liner but during World War II it was converted to serve as a troop carrier. Today the museum aboard the 'Queen Mary' affords a stunning contrast between the lifestyles appropriate in peace and war. On one side of a partition, the tables prepared for high society hold a dazzling array of dishes, crystal and silver. On the other side, one metal tray with indentations replaces 15 dishes and saucers. Bunks, eight tiers high, accommodate 15,000 troops in contrast to 3,000 wealthy patrons in peacetime. To reconstruct the vessel so drastically took a national emergency. The survival of a nation depended upon it. Should you replace your china with metal trays? No! But allow the Holy Spirit to challenge every aspect of your lifestyle.

Our master calls out 'Rescue the perishing!' The captain of the Lord of hosts has trumpeted a 'certain sound' for battle. But the cry of the perishing is often lost in the din of self-survival. While pursuing comfort we can easily ignore Christ's warning in Scripture, 'Whoever tries to keep his life will lose it' (Luke 17:33). We deplore the diseases of the underdeveloped nations: tuberculosis, malnutrition, parasites, typhoid and others. Yet the West has virtually invented a whole new set of affluence-related diseases: obesity, arteriosclerosis, heart disease, strokes, lung cancer, cirrhosis of the liver and more. In saving ourselves we are well on our way to losing ourselves!

Any good cross-cultural training teaches the missionary to adapt as much as possible to the lifestyle of those he is going to minister among—a simpler lifestyle, a lower consumption of goods, a 'make-do and mend' attitude. This forms a solid principle of bonding—establishing a sense of belonging with those he serves.

Those who serve as senders might experience a new sense of belonging and a new vision of their part in 'rescuing the perishing' if they, too, would adopt a lifestyle that approximates to that of those they are sending. Senders who take on this challenge often find that their *quality* of life improves.

A diligent financial support team member must allow the radical challenges of these statements to question his lifestyle:

1) If my lifestyle means running out of money before the month runs out of days, a good starting point might be to ask for help in personal financial management.

2) If my lifestyle means looking into a full wardrobe yet not see 'a thing to wear,' perhaps I should look again at Jesus' words: Do not worry about . . . what you will wear. Life is more than food and the body more than clothes' (Luke 12:22–23).

3) If my lifestyle demands a status symbol vehicle I should check carefully Christ's story of 'bigger barns' (Luke 12:16–21).

4) If my lifestyle roller-coasts on thrills and frills, should turn down the speed and volume enough to notice that life is ready to give free exhilaration through natural beauty (Psalm 19:1–3), fellowship, contemplation and worship.

5) If my lifestyle demands a five-roomed house with sauna, games room and pool, I'd do well to focus on the home awaiting me in the city 'whose builder and maker is God' (Hebrews 11:10).

As we prayerfully consider the Holy Spirit's dealings in our lives we will yield to his will. For 'He who began a good work in you will carry it on to completion' (Philippians 1:6; also see Philippians 2:12 and 13).

God's instructions about money are not 'one-size-fits-all.' There is no hint that Jesus ever told Mary, Martha and Lazarus to dispose of any of their wealth although the record suggests they were quite well-to-do. Yet to the rich young ruler, he said, 'Sell your possessions' (Matthew 19:21).

Although many Christian books only make us feel guilty or tell us to tighten our belts, an excellent book on this subject is *Living More With Less* by Doris Janzen Longacre (see 'Resources', p. 201). It contains hundreds of practical lifestyle changes that encompass every aspect of finance. And it assures you of an enhanced way of life.

Christians with a renewed lifestyle can free up thousands of creative pounds for cross-cultural ministry. Living more with less is an exciting, viable option.

Managing Wealth

Just a cursory glance at the parable of the talents (Matthew 25:14–30) assures us that the Lord expects us to be wise in managing the wealth he has entrusted to us. In a related parable in Luke 19:11–27, he tells us to 'Put this money to work until I come back.'

We can exercise Christian stewardship on two levels: financial practices overseas and financial resources behind the lines.

Financial Practices on the Battlefield

Missionaries could implement plans that include short term, itinerant, Pauline-style assignments instead of strategies that demand costly land or property or other long-term investment. Admittedly, some cross-cultural assignments require a very long commitment—Bible translation, for one. But many mission assignments could be turned over to nationals sooner than they are so that your missionary could move on to new areas of need. A sad but valid criticism is that many jobs still being done by missionaries could be handled more effectively by nationals! Notice Paul's strong encouragement to Titus to 'appoint elders in every city' (see Titus 1:5). His further note, quoting Crete's own poet, suggests Titus was having a hard time finding qualified men—but he was to get on with it! (Titus 1:12).

Self-support

Another practice of biblical times was self-support through the exercise of professional abilities. The developing countries of the world are often in need of our expertise. We can move across frontiers to become residents and take up paid employment (see Acts 18:1–19 for the example of Aquila and Priscilla). Where visa restrictions apply, as they will in almost all cases, make sure before you go that your visa is of the right category, and that your plans are within the law. The opportunities are multiple[1].

Even between the more highly developed countries of Europe, such 'tent-making' ministries should, in theory at least, become increasingly possible as political integration develops.

There are some enviable advantages to this system. It releases financial support for the benefit of other workers, and it puts us in closer touch, cheek by jowl in fact, with those to whom we go; the same living conditions, same work-place, same life-style.

---

1. See 'Out of the Saltshaker and Into the World' by Rebecca Pippert.

There are, however, serious considerations that must be given to this type of ministry[2]. Note in particular that Biblical 'tent-makers' made the spreading of the Gospel very much their priority; professional activities were simply a means towards the fulfilling of the main task. But with the pace at which today's professional world lives, it may prove difficult to keep the 'tent-making' element subordinate. All too readily can the secular responsibilities take up so much time and energy, that the would-be missionary has only the candle-end left with which to spread the light of Christ.

But it is becoming increasingly common for people with independent means to support themselves financially in cross-cultural ministries. Those who have reached retirement age and are in good health—certainly those who have taken or been forced into early retirement—are increasingly able to find fruitful ministries within an established team overseas. Mission agencies are more ready than ever before to recruit and make use of such people, whose maturity in spiritual matters may well more than make up for any lack of experience in the linguistic or trans-cultural areas.

Subordination to local cultural patterns
God, in his sovereignty, is raising up a 'new wave' of missionary thrust, and it is coming from Third World nations themselves. We in the West have for too long thought of those to whom we go as the 'receiving nations'. But wherever national churches have been established the Spirit of God is equipping them too for cross-cultural

---

2. See 'Tentmakers Speak Out' by Don Hamilton.

evangelism. We must work with what God is doing today, and abandon out-dated, human plans which keep ex-patriates at the heart of the operation, and ignore what God is doing in and through his people in the area in question. As one Brazilian pastor was heard to say recently to missionary supporters in the UK: 'We thank God indeed for all you did in sending us the Gospel; we thank God for what you are still doing. But in honesty—and in love—I have to say that some of you are still sending to our old address; we moved, quite some time ago now, and you haven't noticed!'

Paul, the great missionary statesman of the first century serves as an excellent model—again! He was an evangelist. Most often we read of his preaching the Gospel. (There were only a few exceptions—the most notable being his several years teaching in Ephesus). However, he did have a team of teachers (Timothy and Titus are the best known, but there were many others—see Acts 20:4) who were left behind to find faithful nationals and teach them the Word in such a way that they would go out and teach others (2 Timothy 2:2).

Wise and faithful stewardship demands that we be careful not to establish ministries that will forever be dependent on western money. We should not teach methods of evangelism and discipling which require equipment inaccessible in the local situation—projectors, big buildings, expensive books, vehicles, in fact the whole plethora of modern technology. Let the simplicity of the Gospel be clothed in the cultural garb of national people.

There are additional ways of maximising funds for overseas ministries, by careful management of the wealth God has entrusted to us back home.

Financial Resources behind the Lines

Tax Efficient Giving

There are now several ways in which the UK Government promotes and enhances our giving to established charities:

Covenanting:

This is available to ordinary church members, not just to business people and those who make written annual tax returns.

The rules are:

1 A covenant must be signed by an individual—churches and groups cannot covenant.

2 You must be paying income tax. Not all of us do, but it should be remembered that those who live largely off savings and investments will probably be receiving their interest net of tax. If that is so, whether you realise it or not, to that extent at least you are a tax payer.

3 The covenantor pledges to give a fixed amount regularly for each of (usually) 4 years, which can be paid in monthly or quarterly instalments if you prefer. There is no minimum sum although the associated paper work probably means that gifts should be for at least £10 a year. Anything less is not cost effective. The maximum you may covenant is determined only by the amount of tax you actually pay.

4 The beneficiary must be a bona fide charitable organization. You cannot covenant to an individual nor in any way which results in monetary benefit to an individual. (There have been some problems of late regarding the personalized support of missionary personnel, where such funds are not pooled. Societies affected will be able to advise you.)

5 You are required to sign a certificate and give your tax reference, once only for smaller covenants, annually for larger ones.

6   If your financial circumstances change, Christian charities will readily free you from your obligation on request. Should your income in any year during the covenant period inadvertently fall below taxable level, you should simply advise the beneficiaries that you have no tax to pay that year and they will not claim the rebate.

7   A covenant is only in force during your life-time. Your executors face no obligations with regard to it after your decease.[3]

N.B. In the case of those who covenant when paying tax only at the lower rate of 20%, the Inspector, who will be making a rebate at 25%, would be entitled to claim from the donor the small difference. In practice he is unlikely to do so except in the case of sizeable covenants.

The benefits to the Lord's work are evident. At the basic tax rate of 25% the figures are as follows:

A gift of £100 becomes £133
A gift of £250 becomes £333
A gift of £500 becomes £666
A gift of £1000 becomes £1333

So a society whose donors covenant collectively £100,000 per year, will receive a tax rebate of £33,333!

The curious may well ask how it is that 25% of £100 becomes £33. The answer is that in effect you are giving to the charity £133 of your already taxed salary, and the tax you have paid on that part of your salary is added to your gift. 25% of £133 is £33. So you give the net sum of £100, and the £33 tax already paid on £133 of your income is handed on to the Charity by the Inspector, making a total

---

3. See the Government leaflet 'Giving to Charity' No. IR65 available at your local Tax Office.

of £133. A 24% tax rate gives, of course, marginally smaller benefits (which is a good reason why those already covenanting might wish to adjust their covenants upward when the tax rate decreases!)

For higher rate tax payers there is the further incentive that the difference between basic and higher rate tax levels, is deductible from their next tax bill. This means that— with tax bands at 25% and 40%—for a charity to receive a benefit of £10,000, the actual cost to a higher rate tax payer will be no more than £6,000. The covenant would be for £7,500 net, the Inspector would add £2,500 to the Charity and return £1,500 to the donor!

There are some Christians in the UK who oppose covenanting on the grounds that the Church should not allow itself to become dependent on 'Caesar's' money. This argument, with respect, arises from a misconception. As has been shown above, the Government is not adding 'secular funding' to your covenanted gift. It is simply adding the tax you have already paid but which the law does not demand of you. It is therefore, properly understood, wholly *your* money which the charity receives, not some of yours and some of the Government's. If the system used in the United States were used here, no-one could possibly argue that the Church was receiving a government subsidy. Over there Christians put a sum into the Lord's treasury, say US$133, and are then liable to pay $33 less on their next tax bill.

But even if misguided, this reason for not covenanting is at least more understandable than the lame excuses so many of us are left with: 'I hadn't got a form', 'I didn't have a stamp', 'I was too busy to bother!' Or 'I like to keep as far away as possible from the tax man!'

Covenants made easy

Some donors have more reasonable objections. They find the paperwork associated with having several covenants too much, or they do not wish to commit themselves to the same sum every year for the same cause. But nowadays this problem is readily overcome by the use of the so-called 'Discretionary Covenant.'

Trusts which provide this service—there are several4—accept a covenant in their favour for the total sum you wish to give to the Lord's work each year. The tax is reclaimed for you and added to an account from which you can disburse your giving in various ways as often, or as seldom as you like, and for sums as large or small as you like. Your account will be charged with a small percentage to cover administrative costs, but the result is eminently beneficial. A £ 500 covenant with such a Trust might look like this after the first year of operation:

	£ OUT	£ IN	£ BALCE
COVENANT GIFT			
RECEIVED for year one		500	500
DISTRIBUTION to			
Bethany Baptist	200		300
TAX rebate added		166	466
DISTRIBUTION to			
Asian Mission	50		416
DISTRIBUTION			
for Bibles for the blind	100		316
DISTRIBUTION to			
Evangelistic Campaign	25		291
CHARGE for year			
2% of gross sum	**13**		**278**
DISTRIBUTION to			
XYZ project	200		<u>78</u>

---

4 For a list with addresses see Annex II

In this example, your £500 has already produced gifts of £575! and a balance of £78 is still available to give away next year!

Disbursements are made either by asking the Trust to send a cheque to the Mission of your choice or by sending yourself direct a donation voucher (like a cheque) from the supply that they will provide you with. A reminder will arrive each year when your annual covenanted donation is due. The flexibility is enormously advantageous and the system much to be recommended.

Payroll giving

Some sizeable employers are able to deduct gifts regularly from staff wages *before deduction of tax*, for forwarding to the charity specified by the employee. There is a stipulated maximum monthly deduction, the level of which will be modified from time to time. The personnel department will be able to tell you if such a scheme is available at your workplace[5].

Gift aid

This is a scheme by which we may make tax-efficient gifts but of a one-off nature. The system works as for covenants with the exception that it is a once only gift, of not less than £250, during one tax year. But GIFTAID, like a discretionary covenant, can be made to a Charitable Trust for distribution to several causes. It will therefore be particularly suitable for those whose total annual giving would not be less that this but who would be unable to give it all to one organization, or commit themselves to similar gifts every year[5].

---

5. Leaflet IR65 from your Local Tax office covers Covenants, Payroll Giving and Giftaid (also IR113).

Pound-for-pound schemes

Employees of large organizations, such as banks and multi-national companies, may find that their employers give annual donations to charity. Some have set up their own Trusts in order to do so, others have introduced 'pound-for-pound' (or 'matching-gift' schemes) by which they pledge to double whatever gifts their employees make to charity, the employee specifying the beneficiary. Sadly, some employers do not allow religious organizations to benefit from such a scheme, even if registered as a charity. But there can be no harm in enquiring!

Making a will

There are many reasons why one should make a will, not least for Christians is the fact that it gives us the right to determine what should happen to the resources God had entrusted to us after we have no further use for them. To die intestate can cause considerable problems for loved ones, and in the worst scenario can mean that our money finishes up where we would not have wanted it to go.

Wills are often drawn up many years before their provisions become reality, and it is found that inflation has greatly reduced the original intention of the deceased. This can be readily avoided by dividing your estate into percentage shares and earmarking a determined number for the charities of your choice. As the total estate grows, so do the individual shares.

Bequests to the Lord's work in church and mission are free of inheritance tax, so making a careful will can limit the liability of your estate to such tax, and perhaps free it altogether[6]. Making a will—and keeping it up to date—probably warrants legal advice, but there are many books and leaflets you can consult to help you with this essential and altogether worthwhile task. Most Missions can guide you and have suitable clauses available for your use if you wish to leave them a bequest.

Fund raising through sponsorship activity

There can be few in Britain who have not been asked by young people to sponsor them for this or that charitable activity. Cycle rides, half-marathons, swims, fell-walks, parachute jumps, 'readathons', sponsored silences—these and a hundred others have become methods by which young people raise money for good causes. Helping one young member of your congregation to raise enough to spend 6 weeks on the mission field of Africa or South America as a volunteer worker, may seem to some an expensive way of giving a youngster a memorable experience, but it can well issue in a life-long dedication to Christian Mission. Congregations, both at home and in the Third World, have been spiritually renewed in a remarkable way by a carefully planned visit from a short-term volunteer team. It may seem to some to be light-hearted giving and light-hearted going, but in hundreds of cases during the past ten years, it has borne invaluable fruit for Christ. There is now a 1996 Directory available[7] of some of the opportunities offered by over 80 Christian organizations, who will in turn be able to indicate the costs involved.

---

6. Leaflet IHT3 from your Local Tax Office sets out the basic facts about Inheritance Tax and the associated thresholds.

7. Published by Christian Service Centre of Holloway St West, Lower Gornal, Dudley, W Midlands, DY3 2DZ (Tel. 01902 882836)

Gifts in kind

Christians in the United States share excess goods by letting others buy them in so-called 'Thrift Stores'. These are usually stocked entirely by nearly-new goods gifted by Christians and operated by Christian volunteers, though a paid manager has sometimes proved cost-effective. The nearest equivalent in the UK would be our local charity shops which raise enormous sums for a variety of secular charities. There might be room, in a suitable local area, for someone in the UK to develop a similar operation which would dedicate its income to Christian Mission.

A highly effective variation on this theme is already working in the UK, namely the Missionary Auctions[8]. They have raised already close to 1.5 million pounds, from gifts of jewellery, silver or plated items, paintings, clocks, various antiques, general bric-a-brac etc. The income is dedicated entirely to Christian outreach at home and abroad. Many of the gifts have been dug out by Christians across the country from all-but-forgotten corners in lofts and garages; some are unwanted and even unopened gifts! Teams of Christian professionals—valuers and auctioneers—give their time and expertise to make this a highly efficient and trustworthy service. Churches and other groups can unite their efforts to produce various lots for the next auction. Donors are at liberty to specify the charity they want to benefit from the proceeds of their auctioned gift. Says Matthew 6,19: 'Do not store up for yourselves treasures on earth, where moth and rust destroy and where thieves break in and steal.' Surely as Christians in this country, often entrusted with more things of value than we

---

8. For addresses of Missionary Auctions see Annex 1

can reasonably make use of, it is poor stewardship indeed to let them rust and deteriorate when they can be put to the cause of funding overseas workers, or sending study Bibles to pastors in deprived areas of the world.

Interest-free loans

Many UK Christian organizations are obliged to finance their operations with only the smallest of financial reserves. In-adequate cash-flow, especially where monies are subject to delay in international transmission, can prove restricting to the cause of Christ and considerably worrying to missionary executives who have overseas staff to feed. Interest-free loans from their supporters are usually a most welcome proposal. If you need to keep your capital for later use, but would be willing to loan it meantime to the Lord's work—and forego the interest on it—write and ask the Society in question if they would be interested in such a loan and under what terms it could be repaid. You may wish—though it would certainly not be essential—to specify that such a loan would become an outright gift to the Charity in the case of your decease.

The United Kingdom Evangelization Trust will accept such interest-free deposits, the money being totally secured and available for return to the depositor on demand. You may designate the charity to which you wish the resulting tax-free interest to go.

Christian fund-raising projects such as the highly successful Christmas Cracker[9], need considerable capital upfront to get their events off the ground, and may well be glad to return your money immediately afterwards with

9. Christmas Cracker on 0121–6330873

interest—as long as the whole amount is then dedicated to a predetermined charitable project.

And then, when your own giving is done, it should not be forgotten that there are a number of:

Grant–making Trusts

If you have in mind a specific project which requires funding, another whole source of money is available from the estates of Christian philanthropists who have created trusts to finance specific areas of endeavour. It is essential to read carefully the parameters which each trust has set for itself, and not waste trustees' time with applications wrongly or inadequately directed. These are found in the Directory of Grant Making Trusts a copy of which can be found in most local reference libraries. A visit could prove extremely worthwhile.

Investing for the Lord

It is not known what markets the stewards traded in in the parable of the talents, but it is unlikely that they just 'put it in the bank'. Even at 10% interest the master must have gone on a very long journey to double the money. The unfaithful steward was reprimanded for not doubling his! (See Matthew 25:14–30.) Churches in the United States often pool the personal resources of their members so that the investment of 'mutual funds' can bring higher returns for the Lord's work.

UK Christians may feel vaguely uncomfortable about that, but any Christian entrusted with sizeable financial resources should be considering at least every legitimate way of being a faithful and profitable steward. The average church member would need expert professional help on such matters, but there are many organizations set up precisely to give advice to those willing to look for it.

By all means get financial counsel about any of the previous suggestions. For examples of organizations set up precisely to provide such professional advice, see the section on Financial Services in the *UK Christian Handbook*. (If your church has not yet got a copy, do recommend that it gets one—it's a worthwhile investment, which will prove a highly useful tool for all Christian organizations. Otherwise you should be able to consult a copy in your local reference library.)

World economic crises are daily in the news: OPEC nations at a conference table in the Middle East affect our petrol prices. High consumer nations import cheap products from economically impoverished countries while sending back manufactured goods that cost more and more; international companies buy land to produce export crops forcing local people to pay higher prices for their imported food; producers dump grain in the ocean or pile butter into mountains just to keep prices high.

On a scale far greater than we can comprehend, many Christians ignorantly or glibly contribute to the economic injustice of the world, by shrugging off responsibility with a simple: 'But what can one person do?' God's response is in the singular: 'If anyone has material possessions and sees his brother in need but has no pity on him, how can the love of God be in him?' (1 John 3:17 NIV) For even stronger words from the Lord, read Proverbs 24:11–12!

In all the areas we have considered, the influence of one person is small. But it is one by one that we shall stand before him and give an account of our actions: 'wood, hay, straw,' or 'gold, silver and costly stones' (1 Corinthians

3:12–13 NIV). We are to be 'trustworthy in handling worldly wealth' so that the Lord might 'trust (us) with true riches' (Luke 16:11).

A Case Study in Financial Support

The team of senders we have been following are able to rejoice in this area of support:

> Because Lou and Sandy were our church's missionaries, we felt that there was a minimum amount of monthly support needing to be raised by us before we went outside our fellowship for financial support. Early on, Lou had challenged all potential core group members to support this mission financially as concrete evidence of ownership.
>
> Financial support as well as prayer, moral and communication support was raised in this way: First our fellowship was made aware of Lou and Sandy's vision. One Sunday, Lou presented a slide show of a trip he and Sandy had taken to the Philippines several months before to see firsthand several ministry opportunities offered to them.
>
> For the next three Sundays after his presentation, the fellowship inserted into the church notice-sheet a commitment form with several boxes to tick including:
>
> 1) a commitment to support them financially with a space to show the amount and whether it was a one-off gift or monthly;
> 2) a commitment to support them in prayer;
> 3) a commitment to support them with letters.
>
> We had a poster made with the 'Good Ship L, S & M' at one side. It was moveable and acted as the financial 'thermometer.' The 'ship' moved weekly toward its destination as commitment forms came in for Lou, Sandy and Marlies.

Once the minimum amount of support was raised (an amount determined by the society they would be working with), Lou and Sandy then went to family and friends outside our fellowship for financial support.

After all support was committed, support packs were assembled and sent to each contributor. The packet contained:

1) A photo magnet of their family to put on the refrigerator.

2) A 'Coupon Book' with a two-year supply (this was the length of their commitment) of coupons which included the month and a space for the amount of support.

3) Twenty-four envelopes with our church's mailing address already affixed for easy mailing.

So far almost everyone has been great about keeping up with their monthly support. Each month our church sends a cheque to the organization's home office. From there the money is telexed to Lou and Sandy. We've been very blessed! Our fellowship has been so willing to support financially that we haven't had to come up with any unusual or emergency means to raise money for them.

Praise the Lord!

What a blessing it is when people give so that the Good News can go forth. But there is more to the full measure of support needed by your cross-cultural worker. The nickname given to James (the brother of our Lord) was 'camel-knees' from all the time he spent in prayer. Consider the concert of *prayer* support you can offer to God on behalf of your worker.

(In addition to the individual study below, see the **Group Leader's Guide** for session four beginning on page 182.)

For Your Personal Involvement

- Paul had quite a bit to say about his financial support (or lack thereof)! Read each of the following passages and try to determine Paul's philosophy regarding financial support: 1 Corinthians 9; 2 Corinthians 12:13–19; Philippians 4:10–19; Philemon 18–22.

- Do an Old and New Testament word study on tithing. Discover that it is a principle of God's kingdom that works! Include Abraham's refusal to receive money from the king of Sodom, although he was willing to give a tithe to Melchizedek, King of Salem (Genesis 14; Hebrews 7:1–2).

- Without changing your spending patterns, for one month keep a detailed record of your expenditure. Then prayerfully begin listing areas in your lifestyle where there might possibly be unnecessary expense. Use the five statements on page 82 to challenge you in this activity.

- What are you going to do to combat the impact of materialism in your life?

Action Steps

By the time you have read Chapter Four, completed the *For Your Personal Involvement* section and participated in a group discussion, you should . . .

- Decide to purchase Doris Longacre's book *Living More With Less*. Read and apply it!
- Prepare a will.
- Know if you are to be a part of a missionary's Financial Support Team. If yes, let the missionary know of your commitment. Find out where and how to send your

cheque. Let them know the amount the Lord has put
on your heart.
- Involve others. Look for others who have their finances
  in order and wish to see their funds used for the
  kingdom of God.

ANNEX I

Wallington Missionary Auction
20 Dalmeny Rd
Carshalton
Surrey, SM5 4PP
(Tel. 0181-6478437)

Wallington Missionary Mart is associated with the above but handles less valuable, saleable but not auctionable, items at:
105, Stafford Rd
Wallington
Surrey
(Tel. 0181-6693495)

Northwood Missionary Auctions
Freepost
Northwood
Middx HA6 3BS

ANNEX II

Charities Aid Foundation
48 Pembury Rd
Tonbridge
Kent, TN9 2JD
(Tel. 01732-771333)

Macedonian Evangelical Trust
6 Eastmead Close
Bickley
Bromley
Kent BR1 2JG
(Tel. 0181-4678339)

MAXCO Trust
62 The Drive
Rickmansworth
WD3 4EB
(Tel. 01923-710862)

United Kingdom Evangelization Trust
Latchett Hall
Latchett Rd
South Woodford
London E18 1DL
(Tel. 0181-5590114)

Sovereign Giving
(was formerly the North Staffordshire Trust)
6 Heatherwood Close
Thorpe End
Norwich
Norfolk NR13 5BN
(Tel. 01603-700174)

Others are listed in the *UK Christian Handbook*.

Chapter Five

Prayer Support

'And pray in the Spirit on all occasions with all kinds of prayers and requests.'

Ephesians 6:18a

In 1923 a teenager, Helen Mollenkof, attended a Keswick Conference in New Jersey. The speaker was L. L. Legters, who many years later with Cameron Townsend was to found Wycliffe Bible Translators.

God had given Legters a deep burden for all the indigenous people of Mexico and Central America without the Bible in their language. Speaking at the Keswick Conference, he challenged the young people to take the name of one language group in Mexico and pray for that people—that God would open doors so that his word could be translated into the language of their hearts.

Helen Mollenkof was one of those who answered the challenge. She stepped forward and picked the name of a people she'd never heard of before: the Mazahua. She wrote the name on the flyleaf of her Bible. Then, closing her eyes, this teenage girl promised the Lord she would pray for them until they had the Bible translated into their own language.

Helen went ahead with life. She graduated from college, became a nurse and joined the Women's Union Missionary Society. Then she was sent to India, where she served as a missionary for the next thirty-five years. One of her ongoing prayer concerns was for the Mazahua people.

In 1967 Helen returned to the States to retire in Lancaster, Pennsylvania. Some time later, for some unexplained reason, she felt free to stop praying for the Mazahua people.

Then in 1981 she picked up her local newspaper and read an interview with Pat Hamric who, like herself, was a long-term missionary. As she read she discovered to her amazement that Pat, with Hazel Spotts and Don and Shirley Stewart, had been Bible translators among the Mazahua people.

Overjoyed, she found Pat's address and wrote to her: 'I thought you might be interested in my contact with the Mazahua Indians through prayer.'

She told Pat about the Keswick meeting, how L. L. Letgers had challenged them to take the name of one language group in Mexico, and her commitment to pray.

Pat replied, 'The New Testament is complete. It was dedicated in January 1970!'

Helen realized that January 1970 was the very time the Lord lifted her burden to pray!

Most of us are aware of the significance of prayer in God's global plan. We have powerful articles and books on the topic: *An Army of Intercessors: A Concert of Prayer; Seven Minutes with God; Mountain Movers; Praying the Four Ways Christ Taught; Power in Prayer; Destined for the Throne; Effective Prayer Life; Touch the World through Prayer; With Christ in the School of Prayer*.

What is the sum of their message? In the words of Augustine, 'Without God, we cannot; but without us, God will not.'

In his sovereignty, God has voluntarily linked himself to human co-operation. He has inextricably bound himself to the prayer of faith of his children. He merges his working with man's praying.

Though this is a deep mystery, it is clearly revealed in the Word and throughout history. Joshua's day in battle would have gone poorly without Moses' prayer (Exodus 17). Jacob's place in Israel's history would not have been the same without Penuel (Genesis 32). The cross would have been intolerable without Gethsemane (Luke 22).

Today one can stand in the room where John Wesley and the members of the 'Holy Club' held their prayer meetings, a force God used to ignite a revival that was felt around the world.

Consider Evan Roberts and his friends prostrating themselves before the Lord night after night, resulting in the Welsh Revival. Today the Prayer Mountain in Seoul, Korea, gives impetus to the growth of several of the largest churches in the world. The revival sweeping Brazil is evidenced by extra police being put on duty to control traffic in several major cities on *prayer meeting* night!

In no greater arena of human activity is this mysterious union of our prayer and God's work seen than in the mission of the Church.

Jesus was going about all the cities and villages, teaching in their synagogues and preaching the gospel of the kingdom, but when he saw the multitudes, he was moved with compassion. Then he said to his disciples, 'The harvest is plentiful but the workers are few. Ask the Lord of the harvest, therefore, to send out workers into his harvest field' (Matthew 9:37–38). Five verses later, He sent *them* out two by two (Matthew 10:5)!

At the end of time, Christ the Lamb will be extolled: 'You were slain, and with your blood you purchased men for God from every tribe and language and people and nation' (Revelation 5:9). The twenty-four elders singing this new song will be holding golden vials full of incense which are the *prayers* of saints!

Paul in his challenging Ephesians 6 discourse on spiritual warfare not only clearly describes the armour for our protection in war, but also identifies two of the major weapons to use: the sword of the Spirit and *prayer*.

As a missionary of the first century, he was continually calling on the churches for prayer support: 'Brothers pray for us', he simply asks in 1 and 2 Thessalonians. His appeal to the Christians in Rome seems more pressing. 'I urge you brothers . . . to join me in my struggle by praying to God for me' (Romans 15:30). Paul assumed Philemon was on his prayer support team (Philemon 22). To the church in Philippi, he stated his confidence that what he was experiencing would turn out well because of their prayers and the resources of the Spirit of Jesus Christ (Philippians 1:19)—bringing us back to that insoluble co-operation of God and man in prayer.

In spite of all of her lamentable weaknesses, appalling failures and indefensible shortcomings, the church is the mightiest—the only—force contesting Satan's rule in human affairs! And that church on her knees is the purifying and preserving influence which has kept the fabric of all we call civilization from total disintegration, decay and despair.

Samuel Chadwick said, 'The one concern of the devil is to keep Christians from praying. He fears nothing from prayerless studies, prayerless work and prayerless religion. He laughs at our toil, mocks at our wisdom, but trembles when we pray!'

Prayer is not begging God to do something he is loath to do. It is not overcoming God's reluctance to act. It is, rather, enforcing Christ's victory over Satan. It is the effective, fervent communication with the creator of the universe—in line with his will—which controls the balance of power in world affairs.

Prayer transcends the dimensions of time and space and ushers us into the very throne room of God, worshipping, petitioning and interceding in that spiritual realm of the eternal now.

Prayer is sometimes alleluia (Psalm 150). It is sometimes telling God the details of our needs (Philippians 4:6). It is sometimes labouring in unutterable groans of intercession (Romans 8:26). It is the prayer of a sending church that releases power through his messengers in Asia, Africa, Europe and Latin and North America.

Prayer is the arena of spiritual warfare. Those who enter there are in touch with a world in need. Those who enter there regularly know the scars but also the victory of battle.

Prayer is where the action is—supporting and sustaining those working overseas.

It is vitally important for your cross-cultural worker to have a strong prayer support team every step of the way: from her calling to her planning, training, securing financial support and preparing to leave—all before she even arrives abroad.

All Christians are involved in spiritual warfare. Wherever they are aggressively battling against the enemy, there is a greater vulnerability to his attacks. However, your cross-cultural worker often has to deal with battle tactics less familiar than those faced at home. Where there is less Christian witness, there is greater oppression. Cultures more open to Eastern religions and animism are also more aware of the evil spirit world. Territory that Satan has held for generations does not yield easily. Add to this your worker's adjusting to all the unknowns of the new culture, and you already have a sizeable prayer list.

However, because you may never have 'been there,' your worker's prayer needs may seem so remote, so unreal. Thus, you may sense a lack of being able to make your prayer specific.

Here is a prayer list to give you a good start in understanding the areas of special need that make a cross-cultural worker vulnerable to discouragement. When you are in touch, ask which of these areas are vital. And as you affirm your commitment to sustain in prayer your worker will be happy to keep you informed of the more specific requests.

- Adjusting to the new language, different foods, new customs, hard climate.
- Protection in travel, health, accidents, dangerous situations.
- Parents' concern for their children's health, schooling, friendships. Housing accommodation, lack of privacy, differences in living standards, lack of accustomed conveniences.
- Loneliness, homesickness, lack of accustomed fellowship with others.
- Interpersonal relationships, dealing with one's own (and others') prejudice, selfishness, depending on the faithfulness of others to meet one's financial needs.
- Effectiveness in ministry, whatever the assignment.
- Functioning of the tools of ministry. (It is amazing how printing presses break down just when a completed New Testament is ready for printing!)
- Lack of visible results; the 'ploughing, planting and watering' stages can go on for years!
- The people being ministered to, the national Christians, the leaders of the country.
- Need for stability, wisdom, compassion, self-discipline, boldness, power, love, to be filled with the Spirit of God.

A Model Prayer

Jo Shetler had completed the translation of the Balangao New Testament. A flourishing church had been established. She was now called back to the Philippines to be a speaker at the Balangao Bible Conference. Her subject was prayer.

She said that her prayer life had consisted of . . . 'all we ask God to do, such as heal our sicknesses, provide money to put children through school, give the ability to learn a language, translate Scripture and interact well with people.

'Then I decided to pray the prayers of Paul, David, and others in the Bible. I copied them out and started. What a surprise! Those people weren't asking God for the same things as I was! These "model prayers" from Scripture seemed to centre more directly on God and his programme, rather than on people and their plans.'

Read all the articles on prayer; read all the books about prayer. But when you have finished *study and pray* the prayers of the Bible!

One of the prayers of Paul fits perfectly the needs of the cross-cultural worker. He was praying it for the Christians in Colossae, but note how adaptable it is to the needs of any missionary.

Even before he prays, Paul twice assures those at Colossae that he is constantly praying for them. Look at Colossians 1:3, 9: '. . . praying always for you . . . we have not stopped praying for you.'

Everyone who is interested in your missionary will at one time or another breathe a prayer for him or her. Certainly the Financial Support Team will pray, as they write out their cheques, 'Lord, may they use this money wisely', or 'Lord, do they really need this money more than I do?'

The Communication Support Team will no doubt pray that the letters they put so much time into will arrive safely and minister to your missionary.

The Moral Support Team will surely whisper a prayer as they see your missionary's picture on the church notice board or when the pastor leads the congregation in a prayer.

But if you are going to be a part of your missionary's Prayer Support Team, your commitment must be more like that of Paul. 'For this reason, since the day we heard about you, we have not stopped praying for you.'

Here, is a 'model prayer' , from Colossians 1:9–13, that you can pray for your cross-cultural worker:

'Asking God to fill you with the knowledge of his will . . .' (v.9).

Having arrived on the field, a worker is bombarded with an overwhelming array of ministry opportunities. Even if a predetermined job description has been established, there is always one more assignment to fit into the schedule. Joining a team short-handed through illness, furlough, or lack of labourers for an expanding ministry, every cross-cultural worker is faced with appeals to take on 'just a little bit more.'

Out of that mass of good deeds, your worker must discern those that were 'prepared in advance for [them] to do' (Ephesians 2:10).

Once they have heard God's will, a corollary prayer is for them to share judiciously with their supervisor that, in order to maintain sanity, they must say 'no' to certain opportunities.

'through all spiritual wisdom and understanding . . .' (v.9).

It is noteworthy that throughout Scripture these two quali-
ties of the Christian life are always twins—one with the
other. *Wisdom* can be defined as 'the ability to see things
from God's perspective' and *understanding* as 'the facility to
make that godly perspective work out in the affairs of this
world'.

One missionary statesman wisely said, 'The only people
who know everything about missions are those who have
been on the field *less* than six months!' Bombarded with
cultural distinctives, worlds apart from her own culture,
and quite possibly faced with methods that have become
rutted in tradition, your worker continually needs to see
things from God's perspective—things pertaining to family life, ministry, relationship with nationals, economy of
time and energy, finances, prayer–life, relationships with
ministers on the team and those of other groups.

It is not for nothing that Solomon urges: 'Get wisdom.
Though it cost all you have, get understanding' (Proverbs
4:7).

As your prayers bind 'the strong man' (Matthew 12:29),
so your worker can have a clear vision of eternal values,
from God's vantage point, as your prayers elevate your
missionary to be 'seated with [Christ] in the heavenly
realms' (Ephesians 2:6). The worker must now understand
how to make all that happen in the day-to-day affairs of
life.

Days—even weeks—of extended travel away from
home wreak havoc with scheduled family time. Dare we
use God's money to take a holiday? How do I tell the
nationals that we aren't going to use foreign money for

their building—that it is better for the congregation to trust God for the provision? How do I not violate my doctrinal distinctives, yet develop a working relationship with others in the body of Christ? These and a thousand questions bombard your worker's life and demand an understanding heart (see 1 Kings 3:9). To see things from God's perspective is one thing (wisdom); to know how to make them work out in your missionary's day-to-day life is another (understanding).

You can see how this prayer for wisdom and understanding could consume hours of intercession as you wage war against the enemy.

'That you may live a life worthy of the Lord and may please him in every way' (v.10).

Phillips' translation puts it, 'That your outward lives which men see may bring credit to your Master's Name.' Watchman Nee said, 'If you want to be a missionary to China, plan on wearing a "learner's permit" around your neck for the first *ten* years!' Because of diverse cultural distinctives and your cross-cultural worker's lack of ability to communicate deeply, it is often only the love of Christ working out through daily life that tells the Gospel message.

Another perspective of this, of course, is that 'What you are doing speaks so loudly, I can't hear what you are saying!' When your worker's actions differ from her words, it will be the actions that people will believe.

The enemies of the cross gave the name 'Christian' (little Christ) to the believers in Antioch (see Acts 11:26). It was a dirty word then, but since the followers of the Way were 'living letters', known and read by all, they were easily identifiable. Are we so easy to identify?

A team of college students walked into a remote village in Central America where there were no Christians. Their job was to paint a school building a previous team had built. Because they were excited to share the Lord, the weight of their luggage, paint and equipment seemed light.

As they entered the square, they were met by the village chief. He told them his people had heard all they needed to about this man Jesus. 'We don't want to hear another word you might have to say. Just paint our school building as you said you would. We will watch you. When you have finished, we will let you know if we want your Jesus.'

The team knew their outward lives would be living letters 'from Christ, written . . . on tablets of human hearts' (2 Corinthians 3:2–3). All they believed about the word was put to the test in that village.

Those students 'lived a life worthy of the Lord'; when they were ready to leave, ten people including the village chief trusted in Christ as their Saviour!

'. . . bearing fruit in every good work' (v.10).
There are two considerations for prayer here:

1) That your missionary will be involved in 'good work'. Unfortunately, there may be thousands of man-hours of effort that aren't even aimed at decisive points of battle.

Your prayers will release the Spirit's guidance in developing a specific strategy 'in every good work' for your missionary. Your prayers of intercession will open their eyes to decisive points of battle.

2) Thus, being involved in good works, you and your worker are interested in seeing 'fruit that will last.' To give birth to a child is (to say the least) hard work! Yet, the Bible

says 'A woman . . . when her baby is born . . . forgets the anguish because of her joy' (John 16:21). To raise a child in godliness is incomparably more difficult.

To be used of the Spirit to give birth to a child spiritually and cross-culturally is hard work! To nurture that child to maturity demands the patient endurance of years.

It is true that one sows, another waters, but the Lord gives the increase (see 1 Corinthians 3:6).

'. . . growing in the knowledge of God' (v.10).

The personal devotional life of your worker is at stake here. Overseas there are many factors that can lead to spiritual drought:

1) Your worker may become so busy 'working for the Lord' that there is no time for personal intake. Their head can still nod at the appropriate times; their public prayers can still sound almost angelic; their teaching can still be most proper! But the life of the Spirit is gone.

2) Loneliness haunts many cross-cultural workers. More susceptible, of course, are single adults. This can lead to seeking inappropriate relationships, which can lead to spiritual drought.

3) Failure takes its toll of some. High Western expectations are not met. Discouragement debilitates. This downward spiral of morale is as slippery as grease. At the bottom of the slide are many spiritually depleted field workers. Often these burned-out workers do not realize they should go home. They become an embarrassment to the mission endeavour, a drain on the energies of others who are trying to help them and a dismal blot on the testimony of God's church in the world!

4) Disillusionment can bring awful frustration, which in turn may lead to spiritual drought. In the mission process there are many tasks that aren't very glamorous—cleaning the

grease trap outside the kitchen door, keeping an inventory of
radio parts, or being reviled by a drunken street-sleeper.

5) One may, become discontented with other workers.
'Discontent' is putting it mildly! 'Radical interpersonal relationship problems' might be more accurate. This is the number
one cause of missionary failure. Why? Because Jesus said,
'They [the ones your worker has gone out to seek and to save]
will know you are my disciples if you love *one another*' (John
13:35). So here is a major area of attack by the enemy: if he can
destroy our unity he will destroy our testimony!

Your prayers and the united intercession of the prayer
support team for your cross-cultural worker will put a
hedge of protection around them (Ezekiel 22:30), will
guard their thoughts (Philippians 4:4–7) and will give the
wisdom of a peacemaker in those tough interpersonal
situations (James 3:13–18).

'. . . strengthened with all power according to his glorious might' (v.11).

In Acts 1:4 and 8 Jesus gave clear instructions to his disciples to wait for the power of the Holy Spirit. It's a jungle
out there! It is insane to step into cross- cultural outreach
ministry without 'his glorious might'. It is imperative to
have a vital, personal, alive, active, growing, dynamic, real
relationship with the third person of the Godhead, the
Holy Spirit.

Intercede for your cross-cultural workers that they may
be continually being 'filled with the Spirit' (Ephesians
5:18). Pray that they will daily 'have [a mind] set on what
the Spirit desires' (Romans 8). Life and ministry in a second
culture (actually, we *all* walk in an alien world!) hold
challenges foreign to your worker but not to the Spirit of

God. As you pray, the Spirit of truth will guide them into all truth (John 16:13).

'. . . that you may have great endurance and patience . . . joyfully' (v.12).

Joe and Sue were ready to leave Brazil. Because they had stayed several months over the two-year visa issued, the federal government in Brasilia had provided them with a letter assuring them all was in order. However, when on departure they presented that letter and their passports (which showed an expired visa) to the state official, he looked at Joe and said, 'You are in our country illegally! That will be a $500 fine!' Not having the money, Joe and Sue spent three long days, luggage in tow, trudging from official to official until they were finally permitted to leave.

Missionaries, particularly those in Third World ministries, are more than familiar with bank queues, gas queues, food queues and delays in mail deliveries, material deliveries and baby deliveries! Patience and endurance are critical!

But there is another word: 'joyfully'. Yes, your worker might in stoicism realize there is no alternative but to wait. But can they brush off the cobwebs of delay joyfully? Can the joy of the Lord be their strength as after a two-hour wait in line they step up to the telegraph clerk's window to be told, 'Sorry, we are going on strike right now!'?

Yes, your prayers like sweet incense intercede for your worker before the Father day and night, supplying the measure of grace sufficient for any trial. Prayer is where the action is!

'giving thanks to the Father' (v.13).

Paul enjoined the Christians in Philippi: 'Do not be anxious about anything, but in everything, by prayer and petition,

with thanksgiving, present your requests to God' (Philippians 4:6). A thankful attitude reveals a heart that is right
with God.

The pressures of the mission field, however, can produce in your worker something other than a thankful
attitude. The difficult living conditions can say, 'It's not
fair!' The depleting of finances each month can shout, 'I
need more!' The lack of apparent spiritual response can
cry, 'You're not worth my time!' The breakdown in health
can mutter, 'I guess God didn't really call me to these
people!'

Your prayers can be used to challenge your missionary
with Mordecai's words: 'Who knows but that you have
come to royal position for such a time as this?' (Esther 4:14).
Your prayers can be used to help your cross-cultural
worker identify with Paul: 'I consider that our present
sufferings are not worth comparing with the glory that will
be revealed in us' (Romans 8:18). Your prayers can be used
to stir the resources that will build in your field worker an
attitude of thankfulness: 'It is a privilege to be about our
Father's business.'

In-the-Gap Praying

'I looked for a man among them who would build up the
wall and stand before me in the gap on behalf of the land,
so that I would not have to destroy it, but I found none'
(Ezekiel 22:30).

The 'gap' mentioned in Ezekiel has been used to express
a number of concepts. Prophetically Jesus came to bridge
the chasm between God and humankind. As an appeal to
people to go to the mission fields of the world, filling in the
'gap' of front-line workers is critical. There are cultural

gaps between a missionary and the people group they are trying to reach.

But in the context of Ezekiel, 'in the gap' speaks more directly of the role of an intercessor—one who forms a barrier (a wall) between God (who is speaking) and 'the land, so that I would not have to destroy it.'

'I looked for a man. . . .' Abraham became that man: 'God, will you not spare the city for fifty righteous men? Forty-five? Forty? Thirty? Twenty? Ten? Far be it from you to kill the righteous with the wicked. . . . Will not the Judge of all the earth do right?' (See Genesis 18.) Those are powerful words for one who had 'been so bold as to speak to the Lord, though [he was] but dust and ashes!' He stood in the gap.

'I looked for a man. . . .' Moses became that man: 'But Moses sought the favour of the Lord his God. "O Lord," he said, "why should your anger burn against *your* people?' Just four verses earlier, in his anger God had called them *Moses'* people! After two more verses of intercession, 'the Lord relented and did not bring on *his* people the disaster he had threatened' (Exodus 32:11–14).

Another time Moses even more boldly said: 'But now, please forgive their sin—but if not, then blot me out of the book you have written' (Exodus 32:33). Read Deuteronomy chapter nine for a review of the many times Moses stood in the gap for God's people. Moses was definitely an 'in-the-gap' intercessor!

'I looked for a man. . . .' Aaron became that man (Numbers 16). Nehemiah became that man (Nehemiah). Jesus became that man (John 17). Paul became that man (Romans 9). Others through the generations have become men and women who stood in the gap.

And today Scripture still declares the voice of God—which perhaps says to you, 'I looked for *you* to build the wall, to stand in the gap!'

A battle is raging for the souls of men and women. In the book of Job, we have been given some insight into the spiritual realm from which this war emanates.

Job had arrived! He was rich. He was famous. He was perfect and upright. He feared God and hated evil. At least this is what the world could see.

But behind the scenes of this visible world is the real world. And Satan saw the hedge complete—not only around Job, but 'around his household and everything has' (Job 1:1–10). Two excellent novels, *This Present Darkness and Piercing the Darkness* by Frank Peretti, give thought-provoking possibilities to the subtleties of this behind-the-scenes war (see 'Resources', page 216).

The 'accuser of our brothers' (Revelation 12:10) is 'going to and fro' in the earth, and, 'prowls around looking for someone to devour' (1 Peter 5:8). When he sees the break in the hedge, the broken-down walls, the secret thoughts of sin, his entrance to the minds and hearts of men is with ease.

And even when that hedge is complete around a believer, Satan presents himself before God. It's those 'perfect ones' he wants to get. So God, knowing his thoughts, says, 'Satan, have you considered my servant, Job?' (Job 1:8).

This is one of the works of the enemy: to set his heart on even the elect, if it were possible (see Matthew 24:24). Jesus said, 'Simon, Satan has asked to sift you as wheat; but I have prayed for you' (Luke 22:31,32). Satan and a third of the host of heaven who rebelled against God with him are out to destroy to whatever degree and with whatever diabolical consequences they can contrive.

Picture the scene in that heavenly throne room, that secret place you enter boldly to obtain mercy and grace to help in the time of need (Hebrews 4:16). Not only are you and God there as you intercede for the 'mercy and grace' your cross-cultural worker needs, but also present is the adversary. The enemy of our souls is telling the truth about our weaknesses or lying through his teeth about us, using any tactic in his fiendish reservoir to break through the hedge, to rush through the gap.

One of the strongest weapons to bind the work of the enemy is the intercessory, effectual, fervent prayer of a committed, united team of believers.

The Prayer Support Team should never be limited in number. A missionary relates: 'One morning while trying to watch my son's surgery, I "decided" to faint! In the process, I sustained a fractured skull and serious concussion. For three weeks I lay flat in bed and lived from one painkiller to the next. All the missionaries in the area were praying. But one night my wife got on the ham radio to solicit additional prayer from the team back home. She contacted our pastor's wife just as she was preparing to go to a church prayer meeting. Following that burst of intercession, I never took another painkiller. I had no more pain. To God be the glory!'

Unbelief is the single most serious factor that breaks down the wall. God is looking for a team, for a woman, for a man who will 'build up the wall and stand before me in the gap on behalf of the land so that I would not have to destroy it, *but I found none!*' And, in the Ezekiel account, destruction came!

May it not be said of us on that awesome judgement day that he was calling from among us a man, a woman, a prayer support team to stand in the gap, but he found none!

Rather may it be said, 'Well done, good and faithful servant! Come and share your master's happiness!' (Matthew 25:21.)

Fasting and Prayer

In a trilogy of instructions in what has become known as the Sermon on the Mount, Jesus said, 'When you give . . . When you pray . . . When you fast'. He presumes that we *will* fast. He follows each injunction with contrasting instruction: 'Don't do it this way; but do do it this way' (Matthew 6:1–18).

Unfortunately, today what most Christians know about fasting and food is *fast food!*

The biblical significance of fasting, however, is so profound throughout the Old and New Testaments that for us to be ignorant of or indifferent toward its place in a Christian's life is equal to spiritual starvation.

'But I'll starve to death!' is exactly the way many Christians respond. Therefore, we need to know the 'what, why, when, and how' of fasting.

What is fasting? Both in the secular sense and in the biblical sense, fasting means abstaining from food. A total fast is abstaining from all food and drink (Exodus 34:28). A normal fast allows the intake of drink (Luke 4:2). A limited fast indicates restriction of certain types of foods (Daniel 10:2–3).

Why should we fast? Because Jesus told us to. Isaiah gave clear spiritual and physical reasons for the exercise of fasting:

a) Spiritual: 'To loose the chains of injustice and untie the cords of the yoke, to set the oppressed free, and break every yoke.'

b) Physical: 'To share your food with the hungry, and to provide the poor wanderer with shelter—when you see the naked, to clothe him, and not to turn away from your own flesh and blood' (Isaiah 58:6–7).

When should we fast? Definitely not when Christ the bridegroom is around. 'When the bridegroom [is] taken from them; then they will fast' (Matthew 9:14–15). As we still await the return of the bridegroom, *now* is the time for fasting!

How should we fast? Definitely 'do not look sombre as the hypocrites do for they disfigure their faces to show men they are fasting. . . . But . . . put oil on your head and wash your face so that it will not be obvious, . . . and your Father who sees in secret will reward you' (Matthew 6:17,18).

Because our bodies are meant to take in food, and there is no spiritual merit in injuring our bodies through fasting, there are other important 'dos and don'ts' we must consider as we enter and conclude a time of fasting. The finest work on the subject of fasting is Arthur Wallis: *God's Chosen Fast* (see 'Resources', page 201).

When prayer and fasting are practised in concert, they present a unique and powerful duo. Incorporate the practice of fasting with your prayer support.

Prayer for More Field Workers

Jesus left his outreach headquarters, Capernaum. 'Jesus went through all the towns and villages, teaching in their synagogues, preaching the good news of the kingdom and healing every disease and sickness.'

A gruelling itinerary. A heavy schedule. But on one occasion, 'when he saw the crowds, he had compassion on them, because they were harassed and helpless, like sheep without a shepherd.'

Then he turned to his disciples, and said, 'The harvest is plentiful but the workers are few. Ask the Lord of the harvest, therefore, to send out workers into his harvest field' (Matthew 9:35–38).

Having painted a picture of a vast harvest, Jesus shared his means for reaping the harvest: field workers! his harvesters are ordinary human beings who will be obedient to his Great Commission—people who know him sharing with people who don't.

Jesus tells us to pray to the Father that he will send them forth. There is a crying need for field workers today; this is still a most needed prayer. But be careful when you pray it. Remember that several verses later he sent forth the very men he had instructed to pray!

Prayer for an Entrance of the Gospel

Paul solicited the prayers of the Christians in Colosse with these words. 'Pray for us, too, that God may open a door for our message, so that we may proclaim the mystery of Christ' (Colossians 4:3).

Our prayers should be that the gospel—the mystery of Christ—no longer remains a mystery to them, but enters through the door of their hearts.

Often a 'door' that will open into a culture is a story or tradition in that culture which encourages a receptivity to the Gospel. In missiological circles these are called 're-demptive analogies.'

For example, missionary Bruce Olson found that the Motilone Indians of the jungles of Colombia had a ceremony in which they cried for a god to come out of a hole dug in the ground. Olson used this tradition as a bridge to tell the Motilone of the resurrected Christ—who came out of his tomb, a 'hole in the ground'!

Two of the best books on this subject are, *Eternity in Their Hearts* by Don Richardson, and *The Discovery of Genesis* by C.H. Kang and Ethel R. Nelson (see 'Resources,' pages 201f.).

So pray for opening doors as your field workers try to discover redemptive analogies for the people among whom they work.

Prayer to Bind the Strong Man

Paul told the Christians in Corinth that he would stay in Ephesus until Pentecost 'because a great door for effective work has opened to me, and there are many who oppose me' (1 Corinthians 16:9).

Behind every open door of opportunity, there is at least one enemy of the cross—always with a foot stuck out to trip up those who would walk through. Sometimes the enemy is even able to use the actions of other believers to thwart plans!

There is a time to resist the devil (James 4:7). There is a time to cast out devils (Mark 16:17). There is a time to bind the works of the enemy, to bind the 'strong man' himself (Matthew 18:18; Mark 3:27). And there is a time to inhibit his activity and pseudo-authority in the affairs of men (1 John 3:8).

This takes bold men and women praying bold prayers, for the enemy does not like being exposed for the fraud he is.

Prayer for His Kingdom to Come

Jesus said it so simply: 'When you pray, say . . . "your kingdom come" ' (Luke 11:2). Pray for the people into whose lives the kingdom has not yet come.

More than two billion individuals in nearly 12,000 distinct people groups are today without a solid gospel witness, many with no knowledge of even the *name* of Jesus Christ. More than 55,000 die every day without a chance to respond to the message of salvation in Christ.

And we are not talking only about those who live in deep, dark jungles. An evangelist was sitting with his team at the breakfast table of a hotel restaurant in Singapore, a state that enjoys the highest literacy rate in the World and is home to thousands of believers. The group had their Bibles out, and the waitress asked them what that book was. 'The Bible', they told her. Her response: 'What is a Bible?' She had never heard of such a book!

Pray for fallow ground to be broken up (Jeremiah 4:3). Pray for the seed to fall on fertile soil (Matthew 13:3–9). Pray that the waterers will neither drench nor parch the seedling. Pray that the cultivators will not mar the plant by misusing their tools. Pray that the Lord of the harvest will give the increase (1 Corinthians 3:6).

What a privilege that he allows us to participate in his plan of the ages by coming boldly before him, interceding on behalf of the lost of the world as well as for the workers who have gone out to the fields of the world. If God be for us, who can be against us? What an unequal contest it seems!

It is prayer that links the missionary enterprise to the irresistible power of God. Prayer is the decisive point on which the battle turns. The mightiest weapon we can use is the weapon of prayer—potent, powerful, prevailing prayer, the prayer of faith against which the adversary has no effective counter–weapon.

Pray without ceasing.

Case Study in Prayer Support

How does the core group we have been following handle prayer support?

Our prayer support for Lou and Sandy is much harder to talk about than the other areas of support. For example, as regards financial support, we can discuss how we raised monthly support and then have the concrete evidence every month, when the cheques come in, that people are following through their commitment.

But prayer support is a little more difficult. At best we can say how we've tried to encourage people to pray, and how we pray that they are following through their commitment.

One element of prayer support is an awareness of needs. Lou and Sandy's needs are made known in several ways:

1) Everyone committed to support them in prayer is encouraged to have one clock in their house set to Filipino time (16 hours ahead). When we wake up at 6 a.m. and realize that it is 10 p.m. the *next day* in the Philippines, it can prompt us to pray with an increased awareness—perhaps for a good night's sleep!

2) Lou and Sandy have a monthly newsletter they send out to supporters with a specific section summarizing their prayer needs. This portion of the letter can be cut out, highlighted and stuck to the refrigerator with the photo magnet of Lou and Sandy that each supporter received in their initial packet.

3) Two prayer chains have been formed. A prayer chain is simply a list of names and phone numbers. As a prayer request is made known via letter, phone call or fax, the person at the top of the list is notified. They phone the next person on the list who then relays the message to the next person and so on until all are made aware of the need.

Two prayer chains were developed, because it was felt that there could be times when a need would arise of such a personal nature that it might be best if only the core group and a few others determined by Lou and Sandy knew about it in detail. The second prayer chain would receive that prayer request in more general terms. Other requests may be given to both groups.

Another element of prayer support is to be able to intercede as led by the Holy Spirit without even knowing the needs. Or, perhaps, the information we receive about their needs doesn't actually indicate the real needs! It is necessary for us then, by the Spirit, to perceive the real needs as we get together in intercession for Lou and Sandy and the people among whom they're ministering. We're always trying to expand our prayer so we include the people group; Lou and Sandy will be coming home one day, and it seems only reasonable for us to develop hearts for the needs of those people now so that we can keep praying for God's activity among them for years to come.

One way in which we are attempting to increase the efficacy of our prayers was expressed in a recent mailing we sent out to all prayer supporters. In it we asked for volunteers to make a weekly commitment to fast and pray for one hour. We suggested a dinner fast (actually starting right after lunch) with a prayer time following in the evening. We also stated that if they felt led to commit themselves to a longer fast or even a partial fast, that was certainly between them and the Lord. We asked them to make this a four-month commitment and to complete an enclosed form detailing what day they had chosen to fast. This has been on a strictly voluntary basis. The results in terms of commitment will ultimately be seen in a new release of the Lord's power in Lou and Sandy as they go about their work.

There is so much to learn in this area of support. May the Lord grant us ever willing hearts to grow in prayer and may we be ever submissive to get down on our knees and be about our Father's business through prayer.

Prayer is truly a powerful weapon to be used in the spiritual conflicts encountered in cross-cultural ministry. Yet, again, there are other aspects of life to consider. Your worker will also want you to keep in touch through *communication* support.

[In addition to the individual study below, see the **Group Leader's Guide** for session five beginning on page 182.]

For Your Personal Involvement

- Keep a record for one week of the prayers you pray. Is there a good mixture of praise, personal petition, intercession and thanksgiving?

- Study the prayers of several Bible characters. (Be sure to include the tax collector!) Or read through all the prayers of one person. Identify each as a prayer of thanksgiving, praise, personal petition or intercession. Become familiar with the way the prayer sounds. Compare (or contrast) them with your style of praying.

- Locate, read and study the nineteen recorded prayers of Jesus.

- Begin or become part of a missions prayer group where you can learn to participate in the power of united prayer.

- Read Arthur Wallis's book *God's Chosen Fast*.

Action Steps

By the time you have read Chapter Five, completed the *For Your Personal Involvement* section and participated in a discussion group, you should . . .

- More closely pray the prayers of the Bible. Be on guard against the ever-popular 'gimme' prayers.
- Be able to decide if prayer support is a commitment you can make to your missionary. If you can, write expressing that commitment and also your desire to be kept informed of prayer needs.
- Practise the Christian discipline of fasting.
- Pray without ceasing!
- Involve others. Actively look for others in your circle of relationships who have, or who might develop, a heart for prayer.

Chapter Six

Communication Support

'I hope in the Lord Jesus to send Timothy to you soon, that I also may be cheered when I receive news about you.'

Philippians 2:19

'I had no knowledge of missions and no preparation what-soever! I knew God wanted me to go to Paris, but even that was only confirmed in my heart after I arrived there. My home church's "policy" was to lay hands on you, say a prayer and wave, "Goodbye!" My home fellowship group said they would write to me and pray for me. I wrote to them faithfully about every five weeks. I received one letter from them the first year and one the second!

'The results of lack of communication further hit me when I arrived. I was to work with another missionary from my church who was helping equip lay leaders in a new church near the Latin Quarter. When I got there, I found out that he had moved to another city!

'A local national church took me in. I began learning servanthood in a cross-cultural setting. Sweeping, clean-ing toilets, dusting, sorting clothes and running errands were my first assignments. After I regained my ability in the language, I began teaching in their day school for children.

'Lack of communication also hit my wallet! I arrived in Paris with very little money and a promise of a temporary place to stay. (Remember, I had had no training.) I was never taught how to raise financial support. I had not communicated my needs before I left, nor in my letters once I was gone. I thought it was "bad" to talk about money. Now I know I should give full information and allow others to share in Jesus' ministry that way.

'I got a small cheque from a friend through my church the first month. Well into the second month I asked my brother to phone my church to see if any money had come in for me and if they had sent it. Only $45 had come in and that had been sent, returned for postage, and posted again! Anyway, I moved ten times that first year because I had to live wherever I could without paying rent.

'By then I had come to accept it: This is missionary life—until I met Bill and Louise. It began when they offered to help me financially. I felt bad because their church was supporting *them* and they were using some of it to help me. Yet, my church was doing nothing to help me.

'As I got to know them better, I saw that not only were their finances in order, but a whole communication network was in place. Regular mail. Frequent 'care' parcels. Phone calls of friendship (not of desperation, like mine).

'But I really saw how it *could* be when their church's cross-cultural coordinator, John, came to visit them. It was just a one-day visit as he was in Europe on other business, but I saw real caring. He had prepared a special Bible study that he said the Lord had given him just for them. He brought a computer banner saying, "We really do miss you!" It had personal notes scribbled all over it. There were special goodies for their children.

'I came to realize that to the extent that communication, prayer and financial support was strong from their sending church—to that extent their ministry was strong. John said I could call on them any time there was a need. He didn't know the extent of my hurting. (Or did he?) I received a form letter once a year from my church telling me what *they* were doing (Yes, I was even listed as one of their 'accomplishments'!), but they never once asked me how *I* was doing! I had a lot of anger and hurt inside towards my church before coming back, because I felt they didn't care.

'After two years I did come home. And I realized the misunderstanding was as much a result of my failure to communicate as theirs. I was open with my home group. I learned that *they* thought the church was supporting me and *I* thought they knew of my condition and need! We just hadn't communicated!

'I got some good training in communication skills. I learned to be open in sharing my needs for communication as well as for prayer, finances and the other areas of support.

'I am back in Paris, now. No, I don't expect a visit from anyone from my church with banners and goodies. But I do have an established foundation of a strong and growing support team from my home group and other individuals in my church and family. And we're communicating! May God be praised!'

It is hard to imagine the importance of communication from home until you have 'been there'. When a person or family arrives overseas to establish their new routine, real loneliness can set in—a feeling of isolation, of being out of it. A new missionary can feel, 'They have forgotten me!' 'They aren't writing' might be interpreted: 'They don't care! I'm out of their sight—and therefore out of their mind! And I'm going out of mine!'

One family recently returned to Israel, this time with two children. The wife recalls, 'The first two weeks I was filled with guilt for doing this to my children. I had taken them away from the grandparents who cherish them and whom they adore. I had taken them away from *Sesame Street*, a wonderful library, swimming lessons and food they love. I had taken them away from carpeted floors, litter-free parks with grass instead of broken glass, cool weather, Sunday school—from friends, drinkable water that doesn't make them ill, a familiar doctor I can trust, a car instead of a bus or having to walk in the blazing sun and a mother with lots of energy, patience and joy!

'Well,' she says, 'a phone call from Amy back in my home town revealed that she had felt the same way when she first went to Greece. I still wasn't completely convinced that I was doing the best for my boys; but if Amy got through it—and her kids are great . . . and I do trust God who is my Father and theirs, who only wants the best for us. . . .

'After the call, I began to think, "To tell the truth, David and Daniel seem to be adapting more quickly than I am!" Two-year-old David even reminded me of a Hebrew word that I couldn't think of the other day. And Daniel has learned how to fall on these hard floors without getting a big bump on his head.'

The missionary concludes, 'Even my mother is handling this well. She recently encouraged me in a letter: "God wants you there, Mary. Your kids could be ill here, too. C'mon, toughen up!" It seems every time we get discouraged, some bit of communication comes through to *encourage us*!'

Communicating through Letters

Though Paul, the most prolific New Testaments writer, did not have access to the telephone, postal system, fax machines or a computer electronic bulletin board, he knew the importance of personal communication. His letters are shot through with personal comments:

- Requests for his support team to 'bring his cloak' when they come to him and 'especially the parchments' (2 Timothy 4:13).
- An earnest appeal to 'prepare a guest room for me' (Philemon 22).
- In his powerful letter to the Christians in Rome—that great treatise on grace—he devotes almost all of chapter 16 to personal messages. No less than 41 people are specifically mentioned. Tertius, who had been writing the Roman letter for Paul, might have become so excited about all this exchange of greetings that he leaned over and nudged Paul: 'Paul, may I say "Hi," too?' Verse 22 reads, 'I, Tertius, send my Christian greetings also!'

James personalized his short letter 17 times by referring to the dispersed tribes as 'my brothers.' John, when writing to his friend Gaius and again to 'the chosen lady,' found it difficult to put into words all he wanted to say (2 John 12; 3 John 13). Yet in writing his gospel he wanted a scroll the size of the whole world to write everything that was on his heart (John 21: 25). Luke, for the sake of his friend Theophilus, 'carefully investigated everything from the beginning', to set in order the record of the gospel of Christ and the Acts of the Apostles (Luke 1:1–4).

Peter and Paul found it not 'burdensome' to remind their readers again and again of especially important things (2 Peter 1:12; Philippians 3:1). Jude, as he sat to write his brief letter, intended to make it a light, happy rejoicing in their common salvation. But as he took pen in hand, the Spirit of God compelled him to exhort them to 'contend for the faith' (Jude 3).

Whether it be on papyrus, parchment, linen or recycled paper, letter writing is the easiest, most common way of keeping in touch; it is the mainstay of communication.

What to Communicate

The content of your communication is vital. Say things that really matter. Not just, 'How are you? I am fine. Went shopping today. Had meat loaf for dinner.' (Of course, they'll read *anything* from home! But. . . .)

Rather, share your thoughts and feelings—what is really going on in your life. How is God working in you? Be realistic and honest but don't use them as your counsellors. Remember, you are *their* support.

Get involved in their lives overseas as much as you can. Ask questions about their lives there and respond to what they have said in their previous letters to you. This is especially encouraging because it shows that you really read their letters and are interested enough for some follow-up conversation about it.

One sending team member says, 'My wife and I are on the communication support team of over 80 missionaries. We receive 40 to 50 letters every month. When I read their letters, I have a pen in hand to jot down notes or circle specific thoughts I want to respond to. This is the only way we can answer that many letters! And it will work for you, as well.'

Share how God is leading you to pray for them. Ask for their specific and personal prayer requests and updates on things about which you previously prayed.

Share a particularly meaningful sermon you have just heard, church news or news about a mutual friend—edifying news, of course!

When communicating with missionaries serving in restricted-access countries where their ministry may be considered illegal, be sure to check with your church or missionary society for guidelines when writing about Christian matters and ministries.

Encourage your kids to write to the children in your missionary family. This is good training for them to become aware of and involved in missions! Also, grandmas and grandpas, aunts and uncles: keep in contact with your grandchildren, nieces and nephews. They need to hear from you.

Let's look back at the biblical writers referred to for some patterns for you to follow in your letters to your cross-cultural workers:

Paul to the Romans: use names to make the stories real. Instead of, 'Everyone says "Hi!" ' give the names of specific people they know who said 'Hi.'

James to the dispersed tribes: make it a friendly letter, personalized with terms of endearment. Even though (or maybe, because) James had some tough things to say, he reminded them of the personal relationship uniting them. 'Though miles separate us, we are still friends; you are not forgotten' is the feeling communicated when you make the letter personal.

John to Gaius and the 'chosen lady': the time will come when it is tough to sit down and write. You don't know what to say or how to say it. Probably the single greatest hindrance to letter writing is waiting for a big block of time. Don't wait—it will probably never come!

It is not so important to be organized or have nice paper or be able to write pages and pages. What is important is to do it! Jot down a thought or two on any piece of paper. A day or so later when you have another thought, write it down! When you have accumulated a 'letter's worth,' send it! Of course, it would help to number the pieces of paper!

A missionary recalls, 'One of my favourite letters came on John F. Kennedy Airport tissue paper, written while a support team friend was waiting for an international flight! The novelty of it assured me of the instant inspiration of the words written!'

John to readers of his Gospel: don't feel that you have to write every word of every conversation of every friend of theirs for every day they are gone! Allow the Spirit to guide you to share incidents and stories that are uplifting, informative and motivating.

How you say things also has its impact. Consider the following contrast:

'Well, Jerry has taken your place and is doing such a great job with your home group that everything is just fine without you' **vs.** 'Wow! God's timing is so perfect. Just as he called you to Alma Ata, he raised up Jerry to continue the good work you were doing with the home group.'

Luke to Theophilus: be accurate in your reporting to your friends. Distance and time and cultures already have their way of distorting facts. Memory blurs. You want to communicate a true report of what's going on among people at home.

Peter and Paul to readers of their epistles: sometimes with Peter and Paul you will say, 'I do not tire of reminding you again and again to be diligent in your personal devotion to God.' Don't be afraid to encourage and encourage with the same themes and reminders often—as the Spirit directs you.

Jude to those called of God: as you get into the habit of regular letter writing, you will begin anticipating what you want to say. As you listen to the words of a new song on the radio, you realize how they would minister to your friend. You jot them down. As you return to a familiar spot or a favourite restaurant, a pleasant memory inspires you to relate an incident. So you sit down to write, just wanting to rejoice about the good things of life. But don't be surprised if there is also a stirring in your soul as the Holy Spirit says, 'I have an important message for you to share. Warn him to be on his guard for "godless men who change the grace of our God . . ." (Jude 4).'

Other Ways of Communicating

This need for contact with 'home' is nothing new. You remember the story of David, away from his home in Bethlehem. In the heat of battle, he longed for a drink of water from his favourite well over by the city gate (2 Samuel 23:15). His son, Solomon, said, 'Like cold water to a weary soul, is good news from a distant land' (Proverbs 25:25). The need for news from home isn't new at all, but our world has certainly advanced in its methods of communication.

The telephone, for example, lets you call almost anywhere in the world at reasonable cost. You wouldn't use this method as regularly as a letter, but even just once can be a really special treat. You can be led by the Spirit to phone at a time in your missionary's life when he most needs it.

A communicating sender says, 'I was reading a letter from our cross-cultural worker. It wasn't so much what the letter said (it had been written two weeks before) as the

Spirit quickening my mind to understand her present need. I checked the time. It should be about 7 a.m. in Israel. She should still be at home. I called her. On the second ring, I heard her voice. And we talked for a few minutes. What did we say? I can't remember! But she still talks about that phone call that came at just the right time!'

Faxed messages and telexes can communicate with cross-cultural workers if they have access to a fax or telex machine. The work of communicating is still there. But these devices make the exchange of ideas more rapid and convenient. Most recently, e-mail has made it ever easier!

Ham radio is an exciting communication channel. If your worker is in a more remote part of the world, they may know a ham radio operator. If so, ask for the call letters and the times they are usually on the air. Then find an operator in your area. 'Radio hams' are usually happy to set up a 'phone patch' for you to talk with your friend—often free! Around the world!

Communicate through photos. Enclose a photo now and then with your letter. A missionary recalls, 'When we were abroad, we had a wall of pictures of friends and family. After all, it was the only place we saw their smiling faces. It was a lingering point for memories and prayer.'

One of the missionary's sending team adds, 'We have our own wall of cork arranged as the continents of the world. Over a hundred pictures (updated as they send new ones) place our missionary friends in their respective countries. It is for us, too, a place for prayer and memories in our house.'

Videotape is an increasingly popular way of communicating. Your worker would appreciate receiving a video of their home group; of special church occasions; of new members—with a brief interview or introduction. They might also be interested to see a video of anything interesting that's going on in the town.

Adults and children may also appreciate good commercially produced videos, whether sacred or secular. But in any case, do make sure that their machine can handle the videos you send; don't take compatibility for granted.

Send audiotape letters. Just begin talking into the cassette recorder as if you are talking to your friend in person. It is hard at first because there is no feedback. But that barrier of one-way communication can be overcome. And it is refreshing to hear each other's voices as you develop this method of sharing. They can record over the same tape in their response to you.

A 'care' parcel is a great idea. Of course, check first with the post office and with your missionary or society on what may be sent. Find out how to label parcels properly. It is amazing what you can put even in a letter envelope. Find out what your airmail charges plus their duty charges will be; otherwise you might send a parcel that costs double or triple what it is worth.

There are many items that will communicate your love for them: books, periodicals and music tapes, Bible study tapes. One cross-cultural worker enjoys the Sunday sports section of his local newspaper. A loyal friend now sends it every week! From the UK it is possible to arrange for a weekly newspaper 'digest' to be sent airmail almost anywhere. 'The Daily Telegraph' will send 'The Weekly Telegraph' and 'The Guardian' will send 'The Guardian Weekly' for about £1.50 p.w. This is much appreciated. Sometimes even the little things that seem like nothing to us—a packet of salad dressing mix or chilli powder—are a delightful surprise if your missionaries live where those items are not available.

But don't be surprised if their tastes have changed. Ask them what their needs and their wants are now. No matter how mundane the request, if it will minister to them, send it!

Personal visits, of course, are the ultimate in communication. How Paul longed to see his support team. And he thanked them profusely when they sent a representative to minister to his needs (see Philippians 4:15–18, for example).

One church takes a party to Israel each year. Their missionaries in Greece and Turkey have the opportunity every other year to spend this time with their friends from home—in Israel! The church pays the missionaries' fares to come from their place of ministry to Israel for these ten days of fellowship and holiday.

The pastor of one church regularly visits the church's missionaries to put 'new heart' in them and to encourage them in the Lord.

Even if you or someone from your fellowship cannot make the visit, if you know of someone going to your worker's location or nearby, you can encourage that traveller to visit your missionary, and to take a message or parcel of love and concern. On the other hand, if your worker lives at a major crossroads of world travellers, he or she might need protecting from being a perpetual host and tour guide!

Communication support is caring and expressing it; caring *is* communication!

A Case Study in Communication Support

Lou and Sandy's support team makes a special effort to communicate with them:

As my husband and I moved into the home that Lou and Sandy moved out of, we see to their post. Most people send personal mail directly to the Philippines, so we basically collect Lou's magazines, newsletters and other second class mail and a few personal letters that may not be sent directly to them. We mail all of this in a manila envelope once or twice a month, depending on the accumulation. Bank statements, tax returns, bills and other legal papers we hand over to Tim, who is in charge of Logistics Support.

We also send the Sunday sermon tapes in that envelope. Often we include an interesting front page of our local newspaper or Lou's favourite cartoons!

We have also sent care parcels. We try to send special treats for each of them—things that they cannot buy where they live. In each one we include a treat or gift for their host family or the national staff with whom they work.

Because communication is two-way, on one Sunday each month we put up a Philippines Mission table. There is an attractive display with updated information about Lou and Sandy and the mission with which they work. At this table we hand out pre-addressed aerogrammes to people who will write that month to Lou and Sandy.

Apparently there has been no lack of letter communication. In one six-week period, they reported, they had gone only three days without at least one letter, and one day they had received seven!

One month Lou (who is interested in statistical analysis) kept track of the postmarks on the mail they received. (That, in itself, tells us they are getting a good amount of mail!)

Lou reported, 'In checking the postmarks from our supporters to see how long it took for the mail to get to us, we noticed a bell curve based on the arrival of our prayer letter to them. Forty-seven per cent of our communication support team sent their letters to us within a week of their receiving our letter! It pays to write *and* to personalize our letters!'

The ultimate in communication support was afforded Lou and Sandy last summer. Our mission pastor and his family used part of their holiday to visit them in the Philippines. We sent our love along with them in a hundred tangible ways. And they returned our love with thankful hearts.

'Reach out and touch someone', the Bell telephone system used to say. You can still do it through soul-satisfying communication support. But the full circle of supporting your missionary is completed through *re-entry* support as you welcome him back home.

(In addition to the individual study below, see the **Group Leader's Guide** for session six beginning on page 182.)

For your Personal Involvement

- Read one of Paul's letters and highlight all personal messages and comments. You may be surprised how much of his letters dealt with personal communication, logistics and the desire just to convey his friendship.

- Select one of the other letter-writers in the Bible. Identify the kinds of 'ordinary' things he talked about.

- Check with the mission groups of other churches to discover what specific ideas they use in their communication support.

- Talk with missionaries on furlough. Find out from them the kinds of communication support they receive, which are appreciated most and why.

- Review the different methods of communication suggested in this chapter. Which are you particularly interested in? Do you have the necessary equipment for that or those methods?

Action Steps

By the time you have read Chapter Six, completed the *For Your Personal Involvement* section and participated in a discussion group, you should . . .

- Be able to decide if this is the area of support the Lord is directing you into. If so, get out pen and paper now! Write to that missionary God has put on your heart and post it today!

- Prepare a form for father, mother, and children to complete before they go, telling of their needs and wants. Be sure to include a place for their birthdays and anniversaries, types of books they like, music or study tapes they enjoy. If your missionaries are already overseas send the form to them. When they return it, be sure to follow up regularly at least some of their requests.

- Find out what types of things survive in the mail and what things to avoid sending. Find out costs of parcels of various weights and the approximate time it takes between sending and receiving a parcel.

- Involve others. Actively share what you are doing and look for others who might get involved.

Chapter Seven

Re-entry Support

'And they stayed there a long time with the disciples.'

Acts 14:28

'My father was a career missionary. My brothers and sisters and I were born on the mission field. This was our life. Dad diligently directed a theological college for the whole western region of the country. Mother stood faithfully by his side. Our education was as much enhanced by watching their lives as it was by the lessons in our classrooms.

'Through the years they had weathered any number of the storms that assail missionaries. Each brought them to a more determined level of commitment to our Lord and to the cause of training national leaders.

'Tensions between national Christians and missionary leaders were frequent. But my dad was a peacemaker. He could walk that delicate line of cultural sensitivity. Lack of funds became so common that we all knew when to 'tighten our belts'. Discouragement over 'promising' national students who turned their backs on Christian service only toughened Dad's resolve to pour his life into others.

'But probably the most trying experience Dad and Mum faced was the uncertain 'life or death' outcome of his arrest during a military coup. With all the drama of a war film, soldiers barged into our house and took Dad prisoner. They were sure he had 'secret contacts with the enemies of the people'.

'The coup failed. After three weeks Dad was released and resumed his work at the college.

'We kids are grown up now. Several of us are married and back on the mission field ourselves.

'But last summer Dad called us all together for a family meeting. By the curtness of the invitation and his insistence on our being there, we could tell *something* was wrong. In a thousand years we would never have dreamed of what was to take place. The meeting was short and to the point. In essence: "Children, it is important for you to know that I am divorcing your mother. I plan to marry Sue." Sue is younger than I am! His parting words were, "And further-more, I'm not even sure there is a God" '

This tragic story represents perhaps an extreme; yet who knows how different the outcome might have been if the family had had good re-entry support?

In the secular world they are saying it. Re-entry is often the hardest part of an overseas experience and it should not be ignored. There are unexpected problems in return-ing home. Family members who have lived in another culture need to learn how to overcome the difficulties of today's workplace, community and school environments.

In the Christian community they are saying it. Up to 50 per cent of first-time missionaries return home early or don't return for a second term. These wounded people need to identify and process the hurt and anger of failure—to begin to build up their lives again, growing toward mental and spiritual wholeness.

In missions seminars they are saying it. One leader emphasized, 'I have not led one seminar about the drastic need for re-entry help without some missionary coming to me and saying, "I thought I was weird. I couldn't tell anyone about my feelings. Thank you for letting me know that it is okay to feel a little uncomfortable in coming home."

'Recently, just as I finished the re-entry session of a seminar, a woman in the front began sobbing, then weeping uncontrollably. Finally, through her tears, she wailed, "I have been home from Indonesia for three months. Everything you just talked about I am experiencing. Please help me!"'

The Situation of Re-entry

There is an initial *shock* in returning home. Old buildings have been torn down; new ones have taken their place. A favourite park is now a busy traffic junction. Grandma's chair is empty. Your cross-cultural worker probably heard about all these things as they happened. But now that they are home and actually seeing it all for themselves, they are shaken. These factors however are gradually absorbed and accepted.

The *stress* of coming home is another issue. There is a mental stretching as new ideas and ideals are incorporated into the old—which isn't old any more, since that too is new and strangely different.

There is a spiritual pressure caused by the continual memory of the needs of a world lost in sin and what we are or *aren't* doing about those needs.

There is physical stress as well-meaning people stuff their newly returned missionary with junk foods. 'You're so thin; have some more!'

There are odd emotions as perhaps your missionary tries to justify the new and expensive wardrobe of clothes they have just been given. Days earlier, a national had refused to accept a shirt or blouse as a gift, saying, 'I have one to wear while I wash the other. A third one would just be wasted!'

Yes, the home scene with its people, places, and things—all that *you* represent—has changed. But more dramatically, your missionary friend has changed—socially, emotionally, mentally, physically and most of all spiritually. And because these changes happened to each of you so gradually, you yourselves are only slightly aware of them. But as you meet, the changes in each other appear drastic!

Needless to say, the longer your cross-cultural worker has been away, the more pronounced will be the culture stress in coming home.

But even short assignments can produce dramatic changes. The Apostle Paul's entire life was changed in the span of just a few minutes on the Damascus road!

In many situations of world need today, God can instantly open your missionary's eyes to crying needs for ministry. Short-term mission trainers in the USA report, 'For simple exposure to another culture, we have taken people across the border into Mexico and watched God break their hearts with compassion for the lost and needy of this world, in just one afternoon.'

There is another factor to consider in re-entry support: denial. Some workers may prepare to return home denying that they will face any stress upon re-entry. Some steel themselves with the attitude that 'it won't—it can't happen to me.'

Denial can be suicide—emotional, spiritual, mental. And even literal, physical suicide has been the result of some missionaries' shock and stress in re-entry. Your returning missionary may think, 'Look how easy it was for me to adjust to my new culture on the field. What's the big deal? I'm just going home!'

Here are some possible blind spots in that statement:

1) The adaptation probably wasn't as easy in reality as it appears in memory.

2) The months (maybe years) of anticipation before going gave time to prepare for the adjustments;

3) The nationals of the host culture may have been accustomed to Westerners and therefore knew how to help him adapt. In many cultures the people are very gentle, non-demanding and forgiving of missionaries.

None of those factors will cushion your friend's re-entry on returning home. Perhaps unaware, people back home are echoing the same words: 'What's the big deal? She's just coming home!' Because many of them have not ventured beyond the comfort zones of their own world, they have no idea of what a missionary goes through in living and ministering in a second culture. Many supporters feel coming home is basically a non-issue.

Awareness of the factors of re-entry can prepare you to become a strongly supportive friend in the 'coming home' process.

The Challenge of Re-entry

As a re-entry support person, it is necessary for you to keep your eyes and ears open for signs of culture stress in reverse. The returning field worker is the one least prepared to handle the situation. He knows something's not right! The loneliness, the disappointment and let-down, feelings of isolation and not belonging here, the dizzying speeds of everything may find him silently crying, 'Slow down! Slow down!' But it doesn't slow down.

You must take the initiative. You must be the 'intensive care unit' for your missionary's re-entry.

Challenges of re-entry must be faced in any one or more of the following areas:

1) Professionally

After the adventure of an overseas experience, going back to one's old job could be very boring. Equally perplexing could be the 'big-fish-in-a-little-pond' syndrome. Upon return, one suddenly becomes a small-to-medium-sized-fish in a much bigger pond! Possibly the worker will sense an under-utilization of the skills and experiences gained on the field. They may feel the loss of some degree of independence as they work under the more watchful eye of their employer. Or the feeling of being in the old rat race may get to them.

In some areas of work, a year or two away may mean the former job is obsolete. One woman working in computers realized this during her training before she went overseas as a short-termer. Helping her through that stress before she left made re-entry easier for her later. In fact, when she returned, she said, 'I'm not going back into computers. I am working at a nursing home. I see this as a ministry now, and the medical training I'm getting will really open up new opportunities for me to go again where workers are needed.'

2) Materially-Financially

The UK your worker is coming back to is generally much more expensive. That doesn't mean that a loaf of bread necessarily costs more. It does mean that the British spend more money on *things* than do the people of the host culture.

When your cross-cultural workers return, this may cause stress! When they see a teenager go to a full wardrobe of clothes and cry, 'I haven't got anything to wear!' they remember the hours they struggled over how to ask people at home for extra money to feed and clothe local children.

One recently returned missionary said, 'The wealth of this country is very difficult to handle; the wealth of the church is even more difficult for me to deal with.'

Another missionary said, 'It happened to my wife this way: A few months after our return from Mozambique, she was leisurely walking the aisles of a supermarket, choosing this and wisely picking that off the shelves. All of a sudden, she felt overwhelmed. She began thinking, "There are too many choices. I have to get out of here!" She left her half-full trolley there in the aisle, went to the car and drove home!'

Another recalled, 'In Brazil, owing to our various economic and living conditions, *personal ownership* took a back seat in our minds. Upon our arrival home, I began working with a fellow who was using a new Bic felt tip pen. They had not been on the market when we left. He let me use it. I commented to him how I enjoyed the feel of it and how good the writing looked.

'The next day he *gave* me one. "Here, this is yours!" For several days, I would pause and just look at that treasure. "It's mine! It's really mine!" I would muse to myself.'

'Ridiculous!' you might say. Yes, but this is the very level on which culture stress in reverse occurs.

Comparative wealth can begin the stress even before your missionaries leave the field. And children are susceptible as well as adults: Bill and Alice were houseparents in a children's home for Wycliffe Bible Translators in the northern Philippines. Their son William had had an opportunity to spend a week in a tribal village.

Sometime after his return to the Wycliffe Centre, Alice saw William looking into his clothes closet. He was crying. Knowing her own concern for how little they had compared to their lifestyle at home she went to console him. After several attempts at resisting her comfort, he said, 'No, Mum. I feel sad that I have *so much* in comparison to my new friends in the tribe.'

3) Culturally

New beliefs, values, attitudes and behaviour patterns have become a part of your returning worker who may have adjusted to a culture with a slower pace, a more relaxed atmosphere, an emphasis on people and relationships, zestier foods, an afternoon siesta. . . .

The cultural differences that a returning missionary may try to hold onto are innumerable. When schedules and attitudes of people here at home now don't allow for them, he or she feels irritation and *stress!*

One major expectation of most returnees is that people will be interested in their experiences: 'We had been invited to their house for the evening,' one returning missionary wrote. 'We assumed it was to be able to share the excitement of our missionary venture. After a delicious meal during which we were able to insert a few comments, we were ushered into the family room. "Now is our opportunity," I thought. But as our host turned on the TV, he said, "I was sure you would enjoy watching our new 29-inch screen!" I was absolutely devastated!'

What a different story is told of the Antioch church welcoming home their travel-weary pioneer missionaries.

'From Attalia they sailed back to Antioch where they had been committed to the grace of God for the work they had now completed. On arriving there, they gathered the church together and reported all that God had done through them and how he had opened the door of faith to the Gentiles, (Acts:26, 27).

4) Socially

Many people place missionaries on a spiritual pedestal. They are held aloof as if they were right next to God.

'How can we relate to someone who has been a missionary?' they wonder. 'What would we talk about?'

Or some may fear that the missionary is infectious: 'If I have them over for dinner, will my kids catch some kind of exotic disease?' Worse! 'Their enthusiasm for missions might rub off on me!'

It might seem to returning missionaries that everyone is constantly hurrying hither and thither. After spending some time here, one perceptive international observed: 'Here, everyone has a watch, but no one has any time. In our country, few have watches, but everybody has time!'

Compared to much of the rest of the world, life in the West is extremely busy. When your missionary went abroad, their old friends closed the gap created in their lives. Social ties may have been broken with time. Former friends' children have made new friends. Once-dear families may have moved away.

If communication between the missionary and his home church has not been good or if it is a particularly large church, the worker may not even have been missed! One returning missionary who had spent two years of fruitful labour in Europe was greeted by her pastor with, 'Hi, Sally! How was Hawaii?'

One short-term missionary, after returning from a five-week ministry, was welcomed back at church with, 'Bill! You're back! We thought you had backslidden.' It was a blow for the returning missionary since it meant he hadn't being prayed for while on his mission.

There are real situations that may cause stress, but there are also imaginary ones that can be equally distressing. A family recently returned home to their church, which had been kept informed about their mission. The husband said, 'My best friends went sailing by, barely saying hello as if I had only been away for a long weekend. I was mortified! I was distraught!' His friends meant no harm. But rejection, whether real or imagined, can have equal consequences.

5) Linguistically
Your returning missionary has probably learned a second language—or at least some phrases. There are many languages of the world far more descriptive than English. He or she may try to express their meaning in our limited vocabulary and feel inadequate. Stress! They may have 'forgotten' certain English words—which may seem humorous or inconsequential to most of his listeners. Stress! Some of their responses might automatically come out in their second language. Stress!

Further, colloquialisms and slang have changed. Teenagers of returning families might especially feel stressed by not knowing which words are in or out—or even if 'in' and 'out' are in or out! When you see a puzzled look on your returning friend's face, it may be the stress of not understanding current English!

6) Nationally, Politically
A missionary who has been working in a country affected by British foreign policy will have become aware of 'the

other side' of that foreign policy, i.e. how it affects the
people of the country. This may well affect the missionary's political outlook and cause a degree of inner conflict
on their return. They may also feel that they much prefer
certain aspects of the Lost country to what obtains 'at
home'.

7) Educationally

The formal and informal educational standards of the
world vary. Missionary children may for years have been
educated at home or at a boarding school away from their
parents. When they now have to go to a large state school,
parents can understandably be concerned. Children may
feel they are in a devastating situation educationally as
well as socially.

One girl described returning to a school in her home
country. 'We circled the monstrous wood and brick building. We surged forward, carried irresistibly toward its
mouth and stopped momentarily at its gaping door. . . .
I was now in the monster's throat. I felt a downward,
sinking feeling. I was being swallowed! The noise was
like thunder. . . . I was alone in the blackness of that
nightmare.'

That description might fit what any of your returning
missionaries and their children could sense during the
weeks and months of re-entry.

8) Spiritually

Your returning cross-cultural worker's life has concen-
trated on the salvation and discipling of the nations,
knowing God is 'not wanting anyone to perish but everyone to come to repentance' (2 Peter 3:9). They have
become disentangled from the affairs of this world'—

concerned to please their commanding officer' (2 Timothy 2:4). They remember the cry of the widow, the orphan, the lost and dying.

And now, in stark contrast, the demands of a 'godless Christian' society generate stress. There is much to enjoy at home in the U K, yet even that enjoyment can create feelings of bewilderment, anger, guilt and condemnation. The hurt is not only personal; it is also for the hundreds of people left behind in the adopted country who need food and care and Bibles and Bible studies and the multitude of other blessings of the West.

Each of these areas—from professional to spiritual factors—is a stresspoint needing your re-entry support.

Re-entry Behaviour Patterns

Generally speaking there are five different patterns of return behaviour that your missionary friend might manifest. Four of them are dangerous. You need to be alert to the symptoms and help your friend to process their feelings, working toward the expression of the fifth pattern. That is the one you need to facilitate.

1) Alienation
The cross-cultural worker comes home. The feeling that 'I'm only going home!' means they are unprepared for what they are facing. Initially feeling very negative about the home culture, not knowing how to handle what they see and feel, they begin to withdraw.

They make excuses rather than meet people. 'I haven't got my slides together yet,' she says. So she can't share with the home group. 'The crowd at the football match would be too noisy,' he argues. Three weeks later he is *still* 'suffering from jet lag.' These are the types of symptoms you must be on the lookout for. They are shallow pretexts to hide inner feelings.

A person may internalize these feelings and sink further into this pattern of alienation, feeling there is no one to talk to, no one who could possibly understand, no one to help them process their thoughts.

You can pull your worker out of that by inviting them to your home. Just the two of you—or three—is a small, safe number. Or visit some of their favourite spots together—a park, a beach, a restaurant. If they refuse all of this, get desperate! Just arrive on the doorstep and *insist* on some fellowship! Get him or her talking about anything, so that they begin to verbalize their thoughts.

2) Condemnation

This returner is also negative about the home culture. The areas of challenge seem to be overwhelming. He or she didn't realize people would be so unthinking—can't understand *why* the pastor has no time for them. How *could* they be so unchristian! The pressure of this judgemental attitude increases, and they become explosive. Everyone he or she sees knows within minutes how inferior and lacking in spiritual gifts they are—so he or she concludes— because they are not involved in missions. Everything is condemned and criticized from the church pews to Mrs. O'Toole's new hair style.

Be blunt about this condemning attitude. Then let him or her talk to you. This friend, too, needs to verbalize all these frustrations in the safe environment of a close friendship. Don't wait until they feel they must unload in the middle of a Sunday sermon.

3) Reversion

This returner takes a hop, skip and a jump off the plane only to discover people aren't hopping, skipping and jumping any more. Yet they keep trying to deny that any vital changes took place in them while they were gone, or in you who stayed at home. They keep trying to fit in to what was but no longer is.

This person is likely to jump right in to whatever task is put before them. Unaware friends play right into this dilemma: 'So glad you're back! We need a teacher for the sixth grade class!' 'Great! When do I start?' Lead worship on Wednesday night? 'Sure!'

This one will wake up one morning doubting their own sanity. He or she has moved into the fast lane of Western Christianity without allowing time to process the incredible changes that body, soul and spirit have undergone.

4) The Ultimate Escape

Alienation, condemnation or reversion could lead your cross-cultural worker into a devastating scenario of the ultimate escape of suicide—figurative or actual.

The missionary went out to live and minister in a second culture. The experience was good. Language was learned. Relationships were nurtured. Souls were saved. The church was strengthened.

They return, *unprepared* for the changes at home. They try to cope, internalizing all their frustrations. Alienation whispers, 'Nobody cares or understands. Forget them!' The inner voice urges, 'No, I have to get out and share a vision for the world among the church people.' Condemnation thunders, 'But they are so ungodly!' 'This isn't getting me anywhere,' the worker yells back. Reversion reasons, 'Okay, let's just forget it. I was there. You were here. We're back together. No big deal!'

The whirlwind of emotions leaves this person broken. They back out of life—spiritually, mentally, emotionally, or find the ultimate escape is the only alternative.

If you see your returning friend falling into any one of these four behaviour patterns, your help is needed!

The most vital immediate help you can give is to *listen!* Take the time to hear their heart, to share their experiences, to care about their feelings and burdens, to see their slides, to be there when they need someone to talk and laugh and cry with.

The gala reunion parties are fine. But what about at three in the morning: You're awakened by the phone. At first you don't hear anyone on the line. Then you hear someone softly sobbing. You say, 'Sue/Sam, is that you?' There's a weak, hardly distinguishable, 'Yes.' You say, 'I'll be with you as soon as I can!'

Let your friend say anything in the confidence of your friendship. Don't interject, 'I know, yes, I understand.' You probably don't! Just let him or her talk. Encourage them to keep talking by asking leading questions to explain something they have referred to. Ask often, 'And how did you feel when that happened?' Affirm with 'That must have been tough/terrifying/exciting/etc.'

As stability returns to your friend, you can help them move into the fifth return behaviour pattern—the only healthy one: integration. Initially focusing on this means that other patterns are more likely to be avoided.

5) Integration
Integration will take place on two levels: immediate and long-term.

The Immediate

a) Be sure your workers are welcomed and picked up at the airport. Don't overwhelm them with half the church being there, but a good-sized group who will say, 'We're glad you're home!' One church welcoming party arrived at the airport two days *after* the missionary had come home. Fortunately his parents had confirmed the correct day of his arrival and were there to meet him!

b) Arrange somewhere for them to stay. 'And (Paul and Barnabas) stayed there a long time!' (Acts 14:28). It is noteworthy that of the twelve Greek words we translate 'stay' the one used here is defined as *to wear through by rubbing; to rub away!* In other words, their stay with the disciples in Antioch was of such a duration that all strangeness of relationship had come to be 'rubbed away!' When you 'stay' with someone, you know where the extra light bulbs are stored. You aren't just camping out in their house. Whether it is with friends, family, or in a place of their own, be sure to check with your missionaries before they return. Prepare them for the accommodation you are providing for them.

As a church recently welcomed home their first missionary family, the pastor said, 'The washing- machine and tumble-dryer are installed, the water and electricity are on, the fridge is stocked, the telephone's on. I think we're ready!'

c) Have some immediate means of transport for them—a borrowed car or a dependable, inexpensive one that can be sold when they return overseas. One returning woman said, 'Not only did they have a comfortable, dependable car available for my three months at home, but a petrol credit card for my use!' It is important that returning missionaries have some independence and the freedom to be mobile.

d) Provide meals for the first few days. Invite them over; take food in; have their home stocked with some basic food supplies—and maybe a few treats.

But be sensitive. Don't make it difficult for them to say 'No.' Some missionaries have said, 'I can hardly wait to get back to the field. I won't have to eat so much!'

e) Take them shopping. They may not know what styles are fashionable. And they can look conspicuously out of place without even knowing it!

f) Perhaps they had complete medical check-ups just before leaving. If not, ask them if they would appreciate your making arrangements for doctor, dental and eye care visits.

g) After an appropriate few days have a get-together—perhaps a bring and share dinner—so that they can meet more people in a shorter time. A ladies' tea is great for the women to catch up and feel part of things again. But again, be sensitive. They may want to spend most of their time alone for the first week or so.

Long-Term Interaction

Help returned missionaries to integrate their new identity and lifestyle *slowly* into their new environment. They have the opportunity and challenge to be positive change agents—people who can purposefully help all of you at home to see the world more and more from God's perspective. Be open to their new ideas and ways of doing things.

Look for creative ways to help your missionaries introduce global perspectives to your friends. What groups of people could you interest in hearing their report: Sunday service congregations? Sunday school classes? Home groups? Prayer groups? Schools? Other churches' groups? Local radio or TV? A newspaper article? Is their story worth writing a book about?

Allow the creative genius of God to expand your thinking to other ways your missionaries can share their experiences. You can thereby facilitate a good debriefing for them. Paul and Barnabas, on their arrival in Antioch, were given the opportunity to 'gather the church together and report[ed] all that God had done through them and how he had opened the door of faith to the Gentiles' (Acts 14:27).

Scripture further says of Paul and Barnabas that they stayed in Antioch for some time teaching and preaching the Word of the Lord (Acts 15:35). In other words, the time came when they picked up the ministry they had been involved in before going. In due time—if they are not returning overseas—taking up a ministry in the church would be a goal for your cross-cultural workers. This might possibly be in their area of previous ministry. But it is also possible that with their cross-cultural ministry experience, they would now be suited to further develop your church's involvement with internationals who live among you. Or to train new missionary recruits. Or to develop the many aspects of strong sending teams.

Personalizing Re-entry Support.

There may be special re-entry concerns for various members of the family:

1) Husbands can need help.

As a family returns from the field, there are pressures and anxious feelings of responsibility for the husband, who is often perceived as provider. Financial support may have dropped because they aren't abroad now. Yet expenses are probably higher here at home.

Take the initiative in talking about money. Maybe you can help financially, maybe not. But you have helped by bringing the subject 'out of the cupboard'. Let him verbalize the family's needs. Even that may help to sort out priorities. And, then again, it might bring a totally new, Holy Spirit-inspired solution.

Go easy with this, but the time will come to help him talk about future plans. 'What career are you going to pursue?' 'Are you planning to go back to college?' 'Back overseas?'

2) Behind every good man is a great wife!

Abroad she probably played a much more active role in ministry than she will now. Be sure to allow opportunities for her to share. If this is not appropriate in your public gatherings, provide occasions in your living room. Often the wife in the missionary team bore enormous pressures in the balance of ministry and family affairs, and her needs to share are equally valid.

She is pleased with the fully-carpeted, three-bedroom house the church has rented for them. But she is at a loss to know how she is going to keep it clean! More often than not overseas she had a maid who had helped even with the cooking! Help her ease back into the skills of home-making. Be willing to help her with it for a time.

3) Missionary kids are ordinary kids.

Born to British parents but brought up in Japan, Zaire, Cairo or Hong Kong, missionary kids (MKs) often don't know *where* they fit! The UK is their homeland, but it usually isn't their home.

A 14-year-old MK, after returning overseas from a year at home wrote an essay entitled, *What I Would Like to Tell People at Home.*

> I want to answer a few questions I have been asked: No! We don't live in mud huts. No! We don't eat 'foreign' food. It is

very natural. MKs are not perfect. We're human and have faults and virtues like everybody else. When you subconsciously or otherwise treat us as if we should be perfect, we get bawled out by you (who have *no right at all*) and then by our parents (who know better).

No! MKs are not all superbrats. Those few who act like it on furlough are probably trying to hide the culture shock they are going through. No! Just because you're an MK doesn't mean you know your Bible any better than anyone else. All the time when we were on furlough, I was asked to quote Scripture or find something in the Bible I had never heard of. People were shocked and whispered behind their hands.

No! MKs don't go around barefoot and in rags. Mrs. X had seen a picture of me in a paint-spotted teeshirt and cutoffs and assumed I didn't have anything better to wear. Please send money! The money sent to missionaries is never enough! Even though it often appears as if my parents aren't doing anything, they are! And our national friends will tell you so!

How can you support a returning MK? Employ with an MK all the tenderness, understanding, tact, wisdom and patience you would use in being a re-entry support person for an adult.

4) Single and satisfied!

This phrase (the title and subject of a book) might remind senders that single people need special re-entry support, too. Few married people understand single ministry workers' needs of being cared for. And few married couples realize the unintentional insensitivity and hurt hurled at single adults in even Christian circles.

Sometimes re-entry is harder for a single person. At least family members have each other to talk to. Loneliness, perplexities, inability to cope with modern single

relationships and the desire to get on with life can throw
unmarried returned missionaries into quagmires of alienation and depression. You be there to draw them out! Be
there to listen and serve as their 'intensive care unit.'

We are the body of Christ. We are a community of
believers. We need each other. May God challenge you to
become part of a re-entry support team who are serving as
senders!

A Case Study in Re-entry Support

One of the senders team we've been following in our case
studies reports:

> My wife Teri and I are the core group leaders of re-entry
> support for Lou and Sandy. The only experience we have in
> this was the short time Lou and Sandy were with us between
> their field training in Mexico and actually going to the Philip-
> pines. Because their time in Mexico was only three months,
> there didn't seem to be any of the major culture shock or stress
> problems. Still, when they came back from Mexico, we worked
> to make things as normal as possible for them. This was good
> practice for us!
>
> Oddly enough the process started before they left for their
> field training. It began with a commitment on their part to keep
> those of us at home informed of what was going on in their
> lives in Mexico. We were kept up-to-date on prayer needs and
> trying situations in their training and in their 'new' culture.
> We were told about the victories and the defeats. They kept us
> informed about their daughter Marlies and how she was
> growing and how all of them were adjusting to living with
> their Mexican host family. A key to this communication was
> that it was regular. We were 'with them' as they progressed
> through the twelve weeks.

And that paid off. When they got home they didn't have to feel pressured to condense or just hit the highlights of their experiences. And we hadn't missed so many of the little things that had contributed to who they now were. There was already a group of us who had 'gone through it' with them, families with whom they could feel comfortable in rehashing some of their experiences. This detailed debriefing proved as important to them as it was informative to us.

Another aspect of their re-entry support was to attend to their physical needs. Before Lou and Sandy left for Mexico, they had sold most of their household goods and had left their home. So they needed a place to stay for about seven weeks until their departure for the Philippines. Initially there was the chance that they might be able to house-sit for a family that was going to be out of town. As that hope faded and eventually disappeared, Teri and I felt that we should open our home to them. Many factors contributed to our volunteering. We already knew them well and knew that our lifestyles were compatible. The Lord had blessed us with a house large enough for eight to live in comfortably (including a kitchen large enough for both Teri and Sandy). There was an extra room that could be just for Lou and Sandy, while Marlies could sleep in our daughter's room. And, most importantly, we all prayed about it and felt that the Lord was saying, 'Yes!'

We were aware that a lot of people might want to spend some time with Lou and Sandy before they left for the Philippines, so we planned a 'bring and share' lunch after church on their first Sunday home from Mexico.

Because we knew that there were quite a number of their friends who would like to share a meal or spend an evening with them, we decided to keep an appointment/social calendar so that they could budget their time. We prepared a letter that was sent to the other core group members and all support members expressing Lou and Sandy's desire to spend time with those who wished to visit. It also explained their need for time to take care of unfinished business and to relax. The letter was sent out well in advance of their return. Teri acted as their appointments secretary. Lou gave us directions on how full to make their calendar and what days they already had planned for other things.

The rest was simply working with the people who phoned so that everyone could spend some time with them. It made things easier for us and even more enjoyable for Lou and Sandy when we could get a couple of families together at the same time. The letter proved to be successful in that Lou and Sandy were able to accomplish their three goals of seeing people, doing business and relaxing.

The room we were able to provide for them was our den. We rearranged the furniture, brought in a bed and a chest of drawers and put a lock on the door so they could have privacy. They had their own keys to our house so they could come and go as they pleased. Even though they still had their own car, they were free also to use one of ours when they went in different directions.

We have lived with other people at various times during our marriage, but I don't remember it ever being so tension-free. I think the major factor in this good living situation was that Lou and Sandy were doing exactly what God wanted them to do in preparing for the mission field and we as re-entry support team were doing exactly what God wanted us to do. He had prepared all of us to live together—for a while at least. And, as the widow from Zarephath who provided hospitality for Elijah found, the Spirit of God rested on our house.

Though our task will be greater when Lou and Sandy return on furlough, we have learned a lot from this experience. Re-entry support doesn't begin when the cross-cultural worker returns home. It starts before they leave. It continues while they are gone. And *accelerates* when they return. While they are in the Philippines we are keeping in close contact with them so that when they return there will be a group of us who are not 'cultural strangers' to them. We will be able immediately to relate to them as they begin their debriefing.

This then is the full circle of support you can offer to your cross-cultural worker as you express your love and concern for him while he is preparing to go, while he is on the field and when he returns home.

(In addition to the individual study below, see the **Group Leader's Guide** for session seven beginning on page 182.)

For Your Personal Involvement

- Though this aspect of missions life has been long neglected, articles are beginning to appear on the subject. From various missionary magazines collect and read as much as you can about re-entry.

- Talk with missionaries who are on furlough or those who have returned permanently about the challenge of re-entry. But be prepared for some tears! Many missionaries, unless they have had a good Re-entry Support Team, have a lot of bottled-up emotions!

- As you listen to these people, try to identify symptoms of the first four re-entry behaviour patterns.

- Write to the missionary societies of your cross-cultural workers. Ask them for the materials and useful ideas they recommend to help when missionaries return home.

- Write to other missionary societies and ask them for their materials and procedures. Learn all you can about this needy area of missionary support.

Action Steps
By the time you have read Chapter Seven, completed the *For Your Personal Involvement* section and participated in a discussion group, you should. . .

- Be able to decide if this is the area of support the Lord is directing you into.

- If it is, write to the missionary God has placed on your heart. Ask if this is okay with him/her. Find out if there are others who have made this commitment. Begin discussions about responsibilities with the others.

- Four months before your cross-cultural worker comes home, send them material collected on re-entry that will help them prepare for this major transition.

- Involve others. Share the material you collect and all you learn about re-entry with others. Make these people aware of this badly neglected area of missionary support.

Chapter Eight

Your Part in the Big Picture

'Be strong and courageous.'

Joshua 1:9

John was nervous. He had flown into New Delhi only three days before. The noise, heat, dust and thronging masses of people had thrilled him. He was in India, with Eastward Bound, a ministry of Operation Mobilization (OM).

The struggle for prayer partners and financial support; the worries of his mother, who didn't like him going off to such a distant land, were all behind him. He had arrived. He was enjoying the food—not nearly as hot as he had expected—and such a variety.

Now he was going out for his first day of evangelism. He was nervous. He had never been much of a preacher or personal worker. However, he remembered the visit of Gary to his church some months before and the challenge that Gary had given 'to let go and let God'.

Well, he had done just that: surprised himself and quite a few of his friends. But deep in his heart, he knew he wanted God to do a new work in his life.

Of course, he had done some evangelism before, mainly during the OM summer campaign in Europe, which all Eastward Bounders attend before being accepted. But this was the real thing, evangelism in India.

The truck John was travelling in suddenly shuddered to a halt, jolting him out of his dreams. The tailboard crashed down, and the young Indian leader with the big smile told them to clamber out.

Varghese, for that was the Indian leader's name, gently handed him a woven shoulder bag, filled with 'gospel packets'. John learned later that these shoulder bags were made by Christian leprosy patients. The 'gospel packets' were small plastic bags containing a gospel of Luke, a life of Christ, and six different gospel tracts.

'Ek packet char anna,' John murmured to himself. That's what he had been told to say; 'One packet: 4 annas,' 25 paisa, about 2 pence. Incredibly cheap. Highly subsidized by the Bible Society. But how would the people respond?

He and Madhu, his North Indian companion for the day, walked off to a cluster of shops. As they went they heard some of the more experienced fellows on the team start to preach from the tailboard of the truck. John was amazed how quickly a crowd gathered, and how eagerly the shopkeepers in their tiny shops bought the packets.

An hour later, he and Madhu returned to the truck having distributed all of their packets.

It was nearly lunchtime, so Varghese, the leader, decided they should go into a little vegetarian restaurant for their lunch. They ate 'rice plate', rice and a wide variety of little Indian dishes, all for just Rs. 2.00.

After lunch, out again to three other areas of town, and then back to the church where they were staying. As they drove back, some of the brothers started to sing a song in Hindi that John was going to become very familiar with in the months to come: 'Kushi Kushi Mana'.

What rejoicing too. Three serious contacts and a good number of people who promised to send immediately for the Bible Correspondence Course that was advertised on all the literature. Literally hundreds of gospels, several dozen New Testaments and over 5,000 tracts had been distributed that day.

'Thank you Lord for allowing me to come to India and to play a little part in helping these enthusiastic Indian brothers evangelize their own land. I am extremely grateful to you,' a tired but happy John prayed.

OM's Part in the Big Picture

At first glance it would appear that OM is 2000 adults from more that 60 nationalities serving together in over 60 countries and on two ocean-going ships, *Doulos* and *Logos II*. A simple statement of fact.

But as you get to know them better you'll see that Operation Mobilization is an international, interdenominational movement of Christians committed to partnership with the church of Jesus Christ for the evangelization of the world through biblical teaching, a lifestyle of personal holiness and spiritual reality, and by sending out international evangelistic teams who have had some cross-cultural training.

From this diversity of background, wherever you are with OM, one thing is sure—you will see them doing evangelism. Many different methods are used, like literature distribution, drama, coffee bars, children's meetings, open-air outreach, concerts, friendship-building and more. Whatever the method, the goal is to share the good news of God's love.

OM traces its roots to one woman in northern New Jersey who prayed for fifteen years that God would save local high school students and that some of those who found the Lord would become missionaries.

One day she sent a copy of the Gospel of John to a teenager. Three years later, George Verwer, that young man, gave his life to Jesus Christ. In 1957, during their school holiday, George, Dale Rhoton and Walter Borchard drove to Mexico with 15,000 Spanish Gospels in an old lorry. Christian bookshops, radio broadcasts, and the first OM full-time worker, a Mexican, resulted.

In the early sixties the focus of OM spread to Europe, the Middle East, and South Asia. In the seventies, OM's innovative thrust was enriched by two ocean-going ministry and training ships. In the eighties many previously-considered mission *fields* established themselves as vibrant new sending *forces*. And the Muslim world became OM's special emphasis. The decade of the nineties sees OM in partnership with hundreds of agencies penetrating the final frontiers of the unreached people groups.

Since those early days, over 75,000 OM–ers have taken the step of faith to trust God to use them to win people to Christ. Hundreds of OM 'alumni' now serve with evangelical missionary societies throughout the world.

You will not read much more of their history, for OM is a forward-thrusting, looking-to-the-future family of very ordinary Christians bringing hope to the peoples of the world.

Look what God is Doing

Why is it so crucial that you and your fellowship gear up to serve as senders? Because most world Christians believe God is beginning a surge of global activity in our times in which tens of thousands of new missionaries will be going to every people, tribe, tongue and nation. And every goer will need a solid, committed team of senders.

God is doing amazing things in the world of OM. Western nations still top the list of countries sending OM-ers, but the growth areas are definitely the non-Western world. Approximately one-third of OM personnel are non-Western. OM South Korea is a good example. In 1990, OM Korea sent 32 Koreans throughout the world. Today, more than 60 Koreans serve in OM worldwide. The new director on the OM ship *Logos II* is from India. OM India, the largest land-based OM ministry in the world, is led by missionaries from India. On a recent Love Taiwan outreach, 248 participants from 13 countries linked arms with 37 local churches, focusing on evangelism in the three major cities. From India to Indiana, USA, OM India placed 'missionaries in residence' at Taylor University to sharpen the missions vision of students. Albania, that 40 year bastion of atheism, has its arms open to OM workers. OM workers are scrambling to the unending cry for Bibles, literature and evangelists in the newly-formed C.I.S.

In looking toward the year 2000 and beyond, George Verwer, International Director and founder of Operation Mobilization, said:

> I am convinced that by a work of the Holy Spirit, God has given us the privilege of being on the cutting edge of reaching unreached peoples. We are daily challenged to stay on the fine line of what God is doing in the world. There is, of course, also great opposition. As Paul wrote to the Christians in Corinth, 'a great door for effective work has opened to me *and there are many who oppose me*' (1 Corinthians 16:9).
>
> In the light of this battle—this spiritual controversy—one of our greatest needs is to see reality and revival among God's people everywhere. If we are to fulfil the Great Commission we must see a much higher percentage of Christians really get into the action.

We don't just need more organizations, but as new ones are forming, we need to develop a more biblical and balanced view of the ministry of other groups. By being more grace-awakened we will avoid unnecessary controversy (and duplication) that drains us of strength, energy and resources needed for the work.

We don't just need more leaders. But as leadership emerges to move teams through the open doors, we need men and women with a high level of honesty, reality and integrity who will fall on their knees in obedience to the admonitions in Philippians 2:3: 'Do nothing out of selfish ambition or vain conceit, but in humility consider others better than yourselves.'

We don't just need more workers, but they must be the right workers sent forth by prayer in accordance with Matthew 9:35–38. Those workers who come from America, Canada, Great Britain and other so-called developed countries must be willing to live a more simple, sacrificial lifestyle. At present we are transferring too much materialistic Western cultural baggage to the foreign field. It is a counter-productive use of our resources and often a huge stumbling block to people both at home and abroad. It is not just a matter of throwing mud at the walls of the mission field and seeing what sticks. There has to be screening and training; there has to be a discerning of gifts. We need the right people in the right place at the right time. We need more workers with the mind of Christ expressed in the words of Paul, 'Who made himself nothing, taking the very nature of a servant . . .'(Philippians 2:6,7).

We don't just need more churches with resources. But as God is awakening a sleeping giant, the church of Jesus Christ worldwide must make those resources of prayer and communication and finance available. The people of God must have the wisdom and courage and grace to take the risks to invest in this great forward thrust to reach the world with the gospel. They must take the steps of faith to make these resources usable in the hands of all groups who are committed to run the race—who have as their burden reaching these final frontiers—to reach them by the year 2000, if the Lord wills and we will. And if not, in our hearts there is the determination that there will be no letting up until the end—until the Lord returns.

May the Lord help us maintain the love and the balance and the biblical perspective in the midst of all we do in Jesus' name.

The Bigger Picture

OM is not alone in its thinking. Rather, hundreds of organizations are joining hands in the momentous task of reaching the unreached. For God is raising a movement of excited disciples from around the world ready to go anywhere and do anything.

Let's take a world Christian view of what God is doing around the globe today. Here are a few highlights of this final decade of the 20th century—a period in which we will witness (according to many Christian leaders worldwide) the greatest spiritual harvest the world has ever seen:

- The global fellowship of Bible-believing Christians is growing at a rate of at least 70,000 people *every day*.
- 28,000 of those new believers live in the People's Republic of China. In 1950, when China closed to foreign missionaries, there were one million believers. Today, conservative estimates say there are well over 60 million.
- 20,000 of those new-born saints live in Africa. That continent was 3% Christian in 1900 and is almost 50% Christian today.

- 3,500 new churches are opening every week around the world.
- In 1900, Korea had no Protestant church; it was deemed 'impossible to penetrate.' Today Korea is 35% Christian with 7,000 churches in Seoul alone.
- In Indonesia, the percentage of Christians is so high the government won't print the statistic—which is probably nearing 25% of the population. The last accurate tally of Indonesian Christians reported that in 1979 more than two million Muslims turned to Christ!
- After 70 years of oppression in the Soviet Union, Christians number over 100 million—five times the number of the Communist Party at the height of its popularity and 36% of the population.
- The government of Papua New Guinea recently mandated Bible teaching in every school in the country.
- More Muslims in Iran have come to Christ since 1980 than in the previous 1000 years combined. Before Khomeini's revolution in 1979 there were about 2,000 Iranian believers. After years of intensified persecution, there are now more than 15,000.
- In AD 100, there were 360 non-Christians per true believer. Today the ratio is less than 7 to every believer as the initiative of the Holy Spirit continues to outstrip our most optimistic strategies!

(Most preceding statistics are interpretations of data provided by the Lausanne Statistical Task Force. See 'Resources' beginning on page 201, for other statistical sources and update information.)

Where the church has been planted, it's spreading like wildfire. And as it spreads, it's reaching across language, racial and cultural barriers to unreached people groups.

God has raised up Surinam missionaries to go to the Muslims of North Africa, Chinese believers to settle among unreached Tibetans, thousands of Indian evangelists to target the 2,000 unreached ethnic groups within India. The good news is breaking loose worldwide!

And we see only the tip of the iceberg of our heavenly Father's business these days. His perspective is infinitely deeper and broader.

To understand better and find our part as a sender in this awesome task of world evangelization, we must continually look for the bigger picture of God's purpose on earth in terms of bridging cultural distinctives and establishing strong, evangelizing churches where 'Christ was not known' (Romans 15:20).

The Final Frontiers

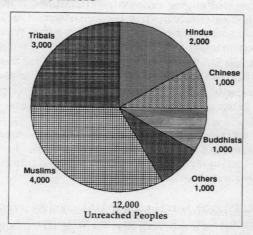

(Source: US Center for World Mission. Used by permission. Graphic artist Richard Endo.)

What is the remaining task? What is the status of the Great Commission in today's world?

- Roughly half of the world's population—actually about 3.05 billion—live in reached people groups. This does not mean all these individuals are Christians; it simply means they live in people groups where it's possible for them to respond to a clear presentation of the Gospel from within their own culture in their own language.
- There are about 2,000 reached people groups in the world.
- In the rest of the world, about 4.4 billion people live in unreached people groups.
- Currently there are about 12,000 unreached people groups.
- While about 1,000 of these unreached groups are scattered among various world cultures, 11,000 of them are mostly in *five major cultural blocs*. These are:

  □ 4,000 *unreached Muslim groups*. Nearly a billion individuals are Muslims.

  □ 3,000 *unreached tribal groups*. About 140 million individuals are in these 3,000 groups.

  □ 2,000 *unreached Hindu groups*. These groups have a population of about 550 million individuals.

  □ 1,000 *unreached Han Chinese groups*. In these enclaves live 150 million individuals.

  □ 1,000 *unreached Buddhist groups*. About 275 million individuals are in these groups.

These 12,000 groups are in about 3,000 clusters which have similar cultural characteristics such as dialects of the same basic language.

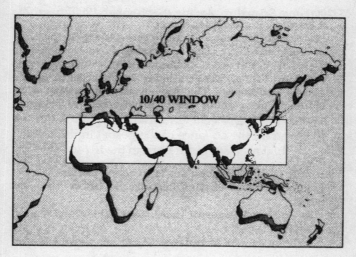

The unreached groups are mostly located geographically in what some scholars call 'the 10/40 Window'—from West Africa across Asia between the latitudes of ten degrees north and forty degrees north.

Within this 10/40 Window are:

    □ most—not all, remember—of the world's unreached peoples;

    □ two-thirds of the world's population, although only one-third of the earth's land area;

    □ the heart of the Islamic, Hindu and Buddhist religions;

    □ eight out of ten of the poorest of the world's poor, enduring the world's lowest standard of living.

Mission statesman Luis Bush, who is calling Christendom's attention to this region, also points out that the 10/40 Window 'is a stronghold of Satan'. He writes in the

AD2000 and Beyond magazine (September 1990, page 7), 'As the Christian presence has expanded around the world, it appears that those people living in the 10/40 Window have suffered not only hunger and a low quality of life compared to the rest of humanity, but have also been kept from the transforming, life-giving, community-changing power of the gospel. . . . It appears that Satan has established a territorial stronghold with his forces to restrain the advance of the gospel in this area.'

The spiritual need staring at us from the 10/40 Window is a staggering picture to look at. Yet, when we grasp its significance, the next question we must ask is: what are we doing about it?

A Mission Renewal Movement

Historically, the modern movements to reach the ends of the earth with God's blessing have occurred in waves. The first wave, championed by William Carey in the late 1700s, washed upon the seacoasts of the globe's continents. The second era, spearheaded by Hudson Taylor about 1865, thrust scores of bold and daring missionaries to the inland regions of the nations.

The third wave, responding to Cameron Townsend and Donald McGavran's call to go to the remaining culturally isolated 'hidden' or 'unreached peoples,' is beginning to swell in this last decade before the year 2000.

As in New Testament times, today there are 'Pauls' and 'Timothys'.

Though fewer in number, there are those who follow Paul's example of 'going where Christ is not named'. They have set bold, adventurous, assertive goals to penetrate the final frontiers. 'But now . . . there is no more place . . . to work in these regions. . . . I go to Spain'—which, in Paul's day, was the end of the earth! (See Romans 15.)

These 21st century, forward-thinking missionaries are taking the Mark 16 aspect of the Great Commission: *Go! Preach!* to every person who has not heard the good news in a culturally relevant context.

On the other hand, there is a second army of cross-cultural workers whose giftings lead them to follow the Matthew 28 command of the Great Commission: *Go! Teach!* Where daring evangelists of previous generations preached the gospel of peace there are today literally thousands of new 'Macedonians' standing on the shores of their nations calling, ' "Come over to help us." Teach us the word in such a way that we will "be qualified to teach others." ' (see 2 Timothy 2:2). It was Timothy, Titus and Erastus whom Paul sent to 'straighten out what was left unfinished and appoint elders in every city' (Titus 1:5).

Some people have suggested relocating the world's 150,000 missionaries from reached fields to target unreached peoples. But much of the work being done among reached peoples is crucial too. Established churches in areas of reached peoples need to be equipped, trained and motivated not only to evangelize their own people but to become sending bases to reach the unreached! Supporting the missionary workers and increasing our financing of this equipping ministry is definitely necessary to strengthen the new churches. These are the new wave of Third World missionaries.

For example, while in port at Arica, Chile, a ministry team from Logos II was sent to La Paz, Bolivia, to conduct conferences to motivate and challenge the churches to be involved in missions. Each night the attendance ranged

from 350 to 1500 people. An average of 100 people each
night indicated their desire to be involved in missions.
Many Latin Americans are being sent as new missionaries
to the frontiers—particularly to the Muslims of North Africa and the Middle East.

Relocating all missionaries to target unreached peoples
is not the answer.

To identify, challenge and mobilize bold, Pauline-think-
ing, world-class teams is the answer to the evangelization
of the remaining 12,000 unreached people groups of the
world. Good news: the task can be done!

We have the Resources

When we think about 12,000 more people groups to reach,
the task can seem discouraging—until we realize the resources God has entrusted to us.

For example, in AD100, there were about 12 unreached
people groups for every one of the existing congregations
of believers. Each congregation would have had to target
12 cultures in order to even begin discipling the nations!
That must have been discouraging!

But by 1950, the ratio had shifted until there were about
33 congregations of true believers for each of the remaining
unreached people groups in the world!

And today the numbers are even more encouraging!

For each remaining unreached people group, there is a
total of 583 Bible-believing congregations (averaging 80
members per church)!

What could happen if 583 churches banded together to
become accountable for one unreached people group such
as the Ewenki of China, the Engenni of Nigeria or the Bozos

of Mali? What would be possible if they put together a church-planting team, if together they provided the prayer power needed, if they pooled resources to provide the home-support of finances, encouragement, communication, logistics and re-entry?

What if just 100 churches committed themselves to reach one people group like the Bozos? What if just ten congregations determined to try out some functional unity enough to link up with a missionary society and reach that people? Or three or two? Or one—your church!

It's not only possible to reach the Bozos and the 11,999 other unreached groups; it is possible to field the necessary church-planting teams within a few years! Missiologists say that we can send church-planting teams to every one of the unreached groups within a seven-year period. To do it, we, the whole church must:

- identify 100,000 new missionaries,
- double our missions giving, and
- pray more—at least a collective hour per day for each new missionary.

God will accomplish his purpose. The gates of hell that bar the unreached peoples of the world can't stand against his church. At the end of time Christ will be exalted with the song: 'With your blood you purchased people for God from every tribe and language and people and nation' (Revelation 5:9). So it's only a matter of *when* and through *whom*.

The fact is that we have more than enough resources to complete the task:

With 500 million believers worldwide, obviously the resources are available. For example, it is estimated that by the year 2000 there will be 83,500 Asian missionaries on the job. In 1980, Korean churches vowed to send 10,000 new missionaries by AD2000; but as they continued their growth rate of 725% per decade, they surpassed that goal in 1995!

We can establish a church movement in every remaining unreached people group, and then help those new believers to evangelize their own people group. It can be done! Will we be a part of it?

It Can be Done. It Must be Done.

We live in a critical hour. The resources are available. Decisive, aggressive action is demanded.

Yet, men have frozen to death lost in a blizzard just five feet from their front door! A whole generation of Israelites failed to 'enter the land' because 'we seemed like grasshoppers in our own eyes, and we looked the same to them' (Numbers 13:33).

Rather, we must be challenged by Christ's strong exhortation to his motley crew of eleven standing on the Mount of Ascension: 'All authority in heaven and on earth has been given to me. Therefore go . . . make disciples . . . teaching them to obey . . .'.

As long ago as 1860, at the great Liverpool Conference on missions, Anthony Ashley Cooper gave a rousing speech which contained his most memorable statement: 'Those who hold the truth have the means enough, the knowledge enough and the opportunity enough to evangelize the globe 50 times over!'

In the 1890s, evangelist D.L. Moody was shouting, 'It can be done! It must be done!'

In that same era of great anticipation for the completion of the task of world evangelization, Bishop Thoburn of

India wrote: 'A century hence, with a world so revolutionized by technology and with the spread of the English language, the final conversion of all nations will no longer seem a far-off vision of a few enthusiasts, and the mention of a million converts will no longer startle timid or doubting Christians . . . a million workers will appear!' (See 'Resources' page 201.)

We are living in that 'century hence!' When we learn of astonishing breakthroughs such as are happening in the C.I.S., let it build our faith! Books could be filled with global events of God's pleasure to uplift his name among the nations. 'Look at the nations, and watch—and be utterly amazed', said God to Habakkuk (1:5). 'For I am going to do something in your days that you would not believe even if you were told.'

Do we believe it? Astonishing wonders are happening before our very eyes. Each day's headlines read like the prophetic fulfilment of God's Word. The world is being evangelized. The nations are being discipled. The Great Commission will be accomplished! The question is: will you be a part of it?

Your Part in the OM Picture

This exciting scenario—the possibility of being a part of the closure of his great plan of the ages—brings us full circle back to you. You are as excited about 'a church for every people by 2000' as any mission strategist who theorizes that it can be done. You are as zealous for a thriving church among the Bozos of Mali as any missionary who envisions going to them. You are as passionate about seeing the lost come to the Saviour as any evangelist. But your zeal has been tempered with the knowledge from God that you are to stay right where you are, actively functioning in your local fellowship.

In this chapter we have focused our attention on OM's part in the big picture of reaching the unreached. Let's superimpose this plan of 'going where the Gospel has not been preached' over the grid of the six sending responsibilities of a support team. What additional activities for involvement will this thrust provide for you?

Moral Support: OM is passionately striving to mobilize God's people across the globe in world evangelization. Over 2000 workers work alongside local churches to share the gospel in four target areas: Europe, the Middle East, the Indian subcontinent and the port cities of the world.

Learn all you can about their work by receiving their various newsletters—*Indeed, Today's India, The Arab World*, etc. For information about your partnership with OM, write to the office nearest you. (See the list of offices on pages 196–197.)

When you hear of a person interested in going to the mission field, encourage them to focus on one of the two thrusts of cross-cultural attack: training Third World nationals to reach the unreached or taking the bold, Pauline drive to 'Spain'. Get into their hands the appropriate literature.

Read Joshua 1. Listen to God's continual encouragement to Joshua to 'be strong and courageous' (v. 6). Again, 'Be strong and very courageous . . .' (v. 7). Yet again, 'Be strong and courageous. Do not be terrified; do not be discouraged . . .' (v. 9). And then, as the people followed God's example (v. 18), you shout the encouragement, 'Be strong and courageous!' This is moral support at its best!

Logistics Support: If you are in a position (formal or informal) to influence the decision-makers of your church, encourage them to establish mission policies that reflect the two-pronged thrust for training and frontier-focus through the kinds of cross-cultural workers and types of missions your church will support.

When missionary candidates come before your leaders seeking support, discern whether they are part of either a Pauline church-planting team ministry to an unreached people or a Timothy, teaching the word to national leaders so they may go out to teach others or develop their church as a sending base. Better, look among your members for the cross-cultural 'parts' and mobilize them to become part of reaching the unreached.

Display prominently literature and posters that encourage reaching the unreached. Any OM office can help supply you. On your church's map of the world, trace the 10/40 Window. Highlight OM work in that area, any missionaries you have working in that area or who are training Third World nationals to go to that area. Border the Window with mirror striping. Let your church-goers see themselves involved in his world!

Financial Support: Until you have a specific friend moving into this type of cross-cultural ministry whom you can support, financially consider directing your missionary offerings to an organization such as OM that is focusing on this massive plan of reaching the unreached. OM has continuing outreach and special projects through which you can invest in the kingdom's work.

You can begin putting into practice the principles of 'living more with less.' You can submit yourself to the discipline of wartime austerity. You can encourage others to join you. These ideas can be effected on a personal and church level.

Prayer Support: To stretch your intercession to include this awesome task, prayerfully adopt one aspect of one target area of OM's work, such as the Manara Book Ministries. Learn about it. Ask for the prayer letters of specific people working in that target area. Understand their lifestyle. Become aware of their schedules, their fears, their rejoicings. Pray knowledgeably for them. Gather a group around you for corporate prayer for them, the people they are ministering among, for the other individuals and churches who with you are supporting them in prayer. And then for the churches that will be established as the result of this God-blessed teamwork.

Learn more about praying for unreached people groups through *Operation World* (see 'Resources' page 201).

Spend an evening at your local library to look up information on the people group your missionary is working among—not just the political country he/she is in. Jot down findings significant to that people's needs, spiritual bondage and possible openings to the Gospel. If the group is already reached and your missionary is equipping them for growth, find out how you can pray that they will become a strong sending base for their own missionaries!

Pray for your church to act more effectively/ positively on the challenge of reaching the unreached.

Communication Support: If you have no friends currently on the mission field, contact the nearest OM office for the names of several workers in a particular target area. Develop a pen-pal relationship with them. One million copies of the *Qur'an* were distributed free in Africa in one year. Contact an OM office requesting information on how you can mail Bibles, Bible correspondence material, books or tracts to pre-selected homes of unreached peoples in various countries.

Re-entry Support: Review our last chapter and remind yourself of the critical needs of missionaries returning from other cultures. Most totally unreached ethnic groups are especially different from Western culture, so re-entry stress is likely to be accentuated in these frontier mission workers.

But the experience they've gained and the unique information they've acquired is particularly important for the home church—for intelligent prayer and strategic planning. Welcome these returning workers into your home and your life. Let them share what they have been learning with your home group or at your church. Have their story written up in your local newspaper. Get them to share in schools and civic organizations. Give them that opportunity for debriefing and for spreading the news of what God is doing in these final hours of history!

If your church has not yet been challenged by the aggressive, forward-thrusting work of OM—bringing hope to the peoples of the world—call your nearest OM office to book a speaker or select a video. Take that first step to opening your church's world to the big picture!

(In addition to the individual study below, see the **Group Leader's Guide** for session eight beginning on page 182).

For Your Personal Involvement

- Read the story of Esther. (It's just a short book.) Pay particular attention to Mordecai's challenge to her when she was hesitant about going in to the king (Esther 4:13–14). As history records, Esther fitted into God's plan and purpose for her. She truly was called to the kingdom for such an hour as that. Throughout

the Bible men and women fulfilled God's will for their
lives and found their place in his Hall of Faith (Hebrews 11). Mordecai's question, reverberating down
through the corridors of time, heard clearly by some
generations, ignored by others, is sounding a challenge to you today—a challenge to recognize that you
have been called to the kingdom for an hour such as
this! It is time to give serious, prayerful consideration:
has God placed a call on your life to serve as a sender?

- Reaching the unreached is such a fast-paced move of
  God that it is making yesterday's headlines look like
  ancient history. Because of this, contact some of the
  organizations listed in 'Resources' pages 182 ff., to get
  current information on global breakthroughs among
  unreached peoples. Be prepared to share those highlights with your fellowship group.

Action Steps

This is it! A decision for personal involvement cannot be
put off any longer! By the time you have read Chapter
Eight, completed the *For Your Personal Involvement* section
and participated in a discussion group, you should . . .

- Be able to decide if serving as a sender is the part of the
  body of Christ that God has divinely established for
  you for right now. You might remember that in the
  very beginning we did say that if not serving as a
  sender is what God shows you by having read and
  studied this book, that is a good decision. Move on
  now to find and actively involve yourself in those
  'good works, which God prepared in advance for us
  to do', for you are 'God's workmanship, created in
  Christ Jesus' for that purpose (Ephesians 2:10).
- If you do sense God's calling on your life to serve as a
  sender but still have not decided on one or other of the

six sending responsibilities—or if you would like to do *everything*, go back over the *For Your Personal Involvement* sections to review each chapter. Find someone who knows you well with whom you can talk, particularly about the giftings and abilities that seem to be the qualifications for each category.

- If you have heard his confirmation and have found one or more areas in which to serve as a sender, actively, aggressively pursue and develop this calling. Begin with the ideas given in this book, but don't be limited by them. Be creative. Expand your capacity to serve. Allow his genius to surge through you for, after all, 'we have the mind of Christ' (1 Corinthians 2: 16).

- Go back to the *For Your Personal Involvement* section of Chapter One, on page 14. If, when you were considering that chapter, you were not able to fill in the statement (p. 16) of the vital importance of serving as a sender, reread those Scriptures and prayerfully complete that statement now.

- Involve others. Having a clear purpose in your own heart and mind, actively seek others in your fellowship who will bind themselves with you in the task of serving as senders. Look for vibrant Christians who don't seem to 'fit in' anywhere. It is quite possible they are looking for an opportunity like this. Share the six sending responsibilities with them.

For 'Everyone who calls on the name of the Lord will be saved. How then can they call on the one they have not believed in? And how can they believe in the one of whom they have not heard? And how can they hear without someone preaching to them? And how can they preach unless they are *sent*?' (Romans 10:13–15).

Epilogue

Serving as Senders barely scratches the surface of your potential involvement in caring for your cross-cultural workers.

Selected resources follow to give you more insight into to this broad subject. But beyond all that you may acquire in your reading is the practical experience you will develop as you become involved in serving as a sender.

We would certainly appreciate hearing about your successes (and failures) as you put into practice the gifts of service God has given you. To God be all glory!

Operation Mobilisation UK
The Quinta
Weston Rhyn
OSWESTRY, Shropshire
SY10 7LT, UK
01-691-773388

OM Canada
P O Box 9
Port Colborne,
Ontario
Canada L3K 5V7
(416) 835-2546

OM Australia
P O Box 32, Box Hill
Victoria 3128
Australia
3-898-9348

Operation Mobilisation
P O Box 914
Papakura 1733
New Zealand
9-298-9990

Operation Mobilization   Operation Mobilisation
P O Box 444   P O Box 30221
Tyrone,   0132 SUNNYSIDE
GA 30290   Pretoria
U.S.A.   South Africa
(404) 631-0432   12-432543

Group Leader's Guide

Chapter One: The Need for Senders
After prayer, summarize the chapter:

❑ From Beth's story, what obviously was wrong?

● Neither she nor her pastor were aware of the critical issue of coming back home.

● Beth was not given (nor did she take) any opportunity to 'debrief'—'to verbalize the depth of her experiences.

● Beth may have overestimated her role in missions involvement.

● Her friends didn't detect the symptoms of the trauma she was experiencing.

❑ Paul was a missionary statesman *par excellence*. Everything we do today to support our missionaries should find its foundation in Scripture.

❑ From Romans 10:13–15, it is clear that those who serve as senders share an equal responsibility and privilege with those who go. (See also John 13:16)

❑ Psalm 139:14 says it succinctly: 'I am fearfully and wonderfully made.' The integrated yet extremely complex personality of your cross-cultural worker will he stripped of every 'comfort zone' he/she has come to appreciate, as he/she grapples with the various stages of ministry experience. Because of this, they need an active, knowledgeable and committed support team while preparing to go, while on the field and when they return home.

❑ What this book is encouraging every mission-minded church to do is being demonstrated by an average-sized church in Sacramento.

Go over the For Your Personal Involvement section:

❑ Help the group see the progression of Paul's linear logic establishing the *senders* as foundational to the goal of the salvation of the lost! It is true that the further one is away from the actual 'action' of one praying the 'sinner's prayer,' the more difficult it is to feel a part of it. Perhaps a couple's experience at being far from the front lines could help illustrate:

'We served for a time with Wycliffe Bible Translators in the jungles of Peru. My wife was assigned to keeping an inventory of the radio parts. For her, a full-time 'people-person', this took some discipline! By tracing the sequence from radio parts to the actual goal of Wycliffe, we were more able to rejoice in such a task. *Somebody* had to keep up the inventory of radio parts so the radio men could keep the plane radios in repair so the pilots could fly the linguists to the village so the linguists could translate the Bible so the indigenous people could have a culturally relevant presentation of the gospel of Christ so they could put their trust in him and be saved!'

❑ Make sure the nine stages and the incidents in time that mark the transition from one to another are clearly understood.

❑ Read the six passages of Scripture that parallel the six support responsibilities. Make sure everyone sees the application of the Scripture.

Pray for those who have committed themselves to a study of this book. Ask the Lord for clear insight into which area of support each should become committed to. Or, if specific cross-cultural support is *not* their function in the Body of Christ, pray that that will be equally clear.

For Further Action

❏ Given the structure of your church, how can you elevate the importance of the ministry of serving as senders?

❏ Do the missionaries supported by your fellowship or by you personally support know of these six areas of service available to them? You might want to consult your missionaries. Get them to place the six support ministries in priority. Further, have them rate on some scale from 'excellent' to 'poor' how adequate they think their support is in each area. Careful! If they are honest with you, what they say may hurt!

❏ From this report, decide on clear, deliberate steps to take in order to reinforce the areas of care they sense are lacking.

Chapter Two: Moral Support

After prayer, summarize the chapter:

❏ From Scott and Jean's story:

- God is not the author of confusion, so obviously some-one 'heard' wrong.
- Commitment as senders is mandatory.
- Support from more than one fellowship is vital.

❏ From the biblical accounts:

- We see how the *lack* of moral support is common in humankind.
- It will take the wisdom of God and conscious effort to reverse the trend.

❏ From the foundation stones:

- Jesus is our example in word and deed as the chief cornerstone.
- Do it simply—and simply do it!
- Moral support is a two-way street.
- Active listening is vital to moral support.
- *Called, counselled* and *commissioned* are watch-words for strong support.

❏ From building awareness:

- There are plenty of resources to encourage and challenge toward moral support.

Go over the For Your Personal Involvement section:

❏ Ask several people to share their meditations on various translations of Matthew 12:20.

❏ Have a 'teaser-length' (1–2 minute) book review of one or more of the books listed or others that have been read.

❏ Identify the kinds of people who can give solid moral support.

❑ Get several people to read their rewritten story.

❑ Discuss some of this world's philosophies—whether by bumper sticker, commercial jingles or other sources of input—that can distract us from giving moral support.

Pray for those who have made the commitment actively to encourage the body of Christ. Pray for those who are still uncertain of their place in ministry.

For Further Action

❑ Contrast Joseph's initial response in Matthew 1:18–19 with Elizabeth's first words to Mary on her visit (Luke 1:39–45).

❑ Role–play various non-supportive, then supportive responses to the following situations: Somebody telling their parents that he/she thinks God wants him/her to go on a two-year mission trip.

Somebody telling their best friend that his/her parents are angry that he/she believes God wants him/her to go on a two-year mission venture.

An assistant pastor is telling his/her pastor that a missionary society has invited him/her to go on a two-year mission venture.

❑ Design your own role play!

Chapter Three: Logistics Support
After prayer, summarize the chapter:

❑ From the story you can emphasize that nobody can do everything. But as everybody does something the job will get done!

❑ Both the Bible and growing missionary society practices are placing the responsibility for initiating the missions process on the local church.

- Identify the cross-cultural parts of your fellowship.
- Give them opportunity to exercise their gifts by being involved in a missions fellowship, by working with internationals in your home town and by going on a mini-mission.
- Check the accountability of the ministry with which they will work.
- Confirm their spiritual maturity and growth before they go, while they are gone, and when they come home.
- Establish good business practices governing all aspects of your missionary's affairs. If your missionary is going through a missionary society, you as the sending church still need to be aware of their policies and where you fit in.

❑ There are innumerable details that can be handled by a group of individuals.

- How should their material goods be handled?
- Are there family matters to be taken care of?
- What ministry needs can be met?

❑ The Body of Christ needs to care for its members by showing diligence, concern for details, punctuality and sound business practice.

Go over the For Your Personal Involvement section:

❏ Discuss how to overcome the strong individualistic tendencies of our culture. How can we become more involved as the body of Christ in each other's lives?

❏ Compile a master list from all the logistical needs each person wrote. Don't be overwhelmed! No one person will have all of these needs, but a list like this emphasizes the diversity of needs and the vitality of Logistics Support.

Pray for those who have made a commitment to be a part of the Logistics Support Team for their missionary. Pray for those who have not yet made a commitment to any area of support.

For Further Action

❏ Consider the last missionary your church sent out. Who in the group knows which and to what degree the various logistical needs of that person are being met by your fellowship?

❏ Consider the internationals who live among us. What loss do they sense in not knowing how to establish all the logistics of 'setting up' in a new culture. What can you do to help them?

Chapter Four: Financial Support
After prayer, summarize the chapter:

❏ From the story you can emphasize God's faithfulness in supplying financial support to ministries he directs. When senders diligently seek God for his direction in helping to support missionaries financially he is faithful to provide the funds—possibly by very unusual methods!

❏ Typical methods of fund-raising do generate some working capital. But for the 'long haul', more basic issues of financial management must be addressed:

Giving. The biblical principle of tithing yields to cheerful giving which grows in obedience so 'there is equality'. Wise giving carefully chooses whom and what to support.

Lifestyle. Living more with less is an exciting, viable option.

Managing wealth overseas. By more carefully supporting economical, *effective* missionary strategy, you free up money for other decisive cross-cultural work.

Managing wealth back home. This is kinder and gentler to the environment as well as freeing up funds for missions!

Go over the For Your Personal Involvement section:

❏ From Scripture, discuss the philosophy of financial support the Apostle Paul seems to have adopted.

❏ Tithing is one principle of the kingdom of God. It works!

❏ Encourage discussion about the five propositions on page 75. Avoid condemnation either of yourselves or others; however, allow the Holy Spirit his opportunity to convict in the area of *our* wealth.

❏ Media input first *sells* us our *needs*, then provides us with the plastic money to mortgage our future.

Pray for those who have made a commitment to be a part of a missionary's Financial Support Team and for those who are still uncertain as to their personal involvement in serving as a sender.

For Further Action

❑ Do a study on the financial accountability of the organizations with which your missionaries are working.

❑ Do a study on the financial accountability of your missionaries.

Chapter Five: Prayer Support
After prayer, summarize the chapter:

❑ From Helen Mollenkof's story, it is clear that commitment to prayer is not to be lightly regarded; rather, it is a discipline of long-term obedience.

❑ Though the efficacy of prayer is a divine mystery, the practice of prayer is as clear as any Bible story.

❑ Prayer is the arena of spiritual warfare. Only the well-advised should enter there.

❑ The prayers of the Bible can serve as models for our prayers. These prayers provide for us the language and nature of petitions in line with the heart of God.

❑ Prayer with *fasting* is a powerful weapon in the spiritual warfare we are facing with our cross-cultural worker.

❑ 'In-the-gap' praying is a level of intercession that demands a depth of commitment beyond the novice.

❑ 'The harvest is plentiful but the workers are few' is as true today as when Jesus spoke it. Therefore, 'Ask the Lord of the harvest to send out workers' (Matthew 9:37–38).

❑ Pray that the gospel, in a culturally-relevant context, will be presented to all peoples.

❑ Pray that the 'strong man' will be bound.

❑ Pray for the coming of God's kingdom to the hearts of all people.

Go over the For Your Personal Involvement section:

❑ Discuss the types of prayers the group has been used to praying.

❑ Discuss several model prayers of Jesus and other Bible characters that have been studied, and what differences the group anticipates in their praying now.

❑ Ask someone to prepare and give a book review of *God's Chosen Fast* (see 'Resources', page 201).

❑ Have available the addresses of your church's missionaries for those who are ready to make a commitment to their prayer support.

Pray for those who have made a commitment to be a part of a cross-cultural worker's Prayer Support Team. Pray for those who have yet to make a commitment to any area of support.

For Further Action

❑ Begin a mission prayer group, or increase awareness of the existing one(s).

❑ Give a more prominent visual place to the prayer requests of your missionaries by

- Posting letters on the church notice board with prayer requests highlighted.
- Putting excerpts of those requests in the church notice sheet each week or month.
- Requesting regular public congregational prayer for specific needs of your missionaries.

❑ Expand the vision of your church's outreach by using a world prayer guide such as the *Global Prayer Digest, Passport* booklets, 'Unreached People Profiles' and *Operation World* (see 'Resources', pages 200, 203, 204.)

❑ Prayer support is the most vital of the six areas.

- History tells of many who forged their way to God's chosen fields of the world without *Moral Support*. But they got there.
- Having one or more friends back home handling all of the *Logistics Support* eases the mind of the cross-cultural worker. But they have survived without it.
- *Financial Support* does provide conveniently for the worker's needs. But the belt can be tightened.
- News from a far country provides great *Communication Support*. But loneliness can be handled.

- *Re-entry Support* certainly shores up the unstable as they come back home. But life goes on.

These five areas of support relate to the physical, emotional and psychological realms. Though the adjustments for lack of support in these areas are difficult, they can be made.

However, *Prayer Support* moves into the realm of the spiritual *where there is no adjustment for lack of support!* Therefore, make this issue the highest priority.

Chapter Six: Communication Support
After prayer, summarize the chapter:

❑ From the Paris missionary's story:
- God is merciful, but there is a better part of wisdom that says missionaries should get some good, practical training.
- Working with nationals enabled her to stay in the country.
- It was fortunate for her to see a positive example.

❑ From Mary's story:
- Even returning missionaries face difficulties that are helped by communication support.
- The encouragement of communication support doesn't always take away the difficulty, but it certainly helps your missionary through it.

❑ From the biblical writers:
- Make the communication real.
- Be personal.
- Even short letters should be written and sent.
- Communication support is for *their* benefit.
- Don't feel you have to say everything you know.
- Reminders are good.
- Sometimes your communication might be a God-inspired exhortation.

❑ Get everyone involved in letter writing.

❑ Be sure the content is worth reading.

❑ Use other means of communication as appropriate
- Telephone, fax, e-mail, telex, ham radio, photos, video, audiotapes, care parcels, visits.

Go over the For Your Personal Involvement section:

❑ Get several people to share their highlighted letter of Paul. What was mundane in the letter—yet important enough to be included in Scripture? What did some of the other writers talk about?

❑ Make a list as the group relates the many different types of communication support missionaries have received.

❑ What have other churches found to be practical ways towards communication support?

❑ Compile a list of the resources within your group for communication support.

Pray for those who have made the commitment to be a part of a missionary's Communication Support Team. Pray for those who have not yet made a decision regarding any area of support.

For Further Action

❑ Give each person present a half sheet of paper to write a personal note to your missionary. Gather them into one envelope and post it—*tonight!*

❑ Prepare a chart to show what time it is where your missionary is living and the best times to reach him/her by telephone—if they have a telephone.

❑ Talk with the children's leader or Sunday school superintendent. Develop a plan for children to write to missionary children in other countries.

Chapter Seven: Re-entry Support
After prayer, summarize the chapter:

❑ From the seminary director's story:
- The devastation of this missionary's 'crash' spreads far beyond the circle of his immediate family.
- No doubt many factors beyond re-entry stress contributed to his 'spiritual suicide'. But *if* he had had a good Re-entry Support Team to unload on, what grief might have been averted!

❑ From the Situation of Re-entry:
- Re-entry *shock* is the initial response and deals more with environmental changes your worker must face.
- Re-entry *stress* deals more with the deeper struggles of attitude and spiritual motivation that run contrary in the two cultures.

❑ From the Challenge of Re-entry:
- Become very familiar with these eight areas. It is in one or more of them that you will sense some struggle in your returning cross-cultural worker.
- Know your worker well. Think beyond the examples given to specific issues that might frustrate him/her upon re-entry.

❑ From the Re-entry Behaviour Patterns:
- Alienation, condemnation and reversion sometimes provide the degenerative spiral down to the fourth, the ultimate escape. Be aware of these and if you notice the signs, try to divert the returned missionary from this destruction.
- The focus of your re-entry programme should be on the fifth pattern: *Integration!*
- Integration is on two levels: the immediate needs of living and long-range interaction.
- The most vital, immediate issue on either level is the need for active listening.

- The Re-entry Support Team must provide opportunities for debriefing. This is as much for your worker's benefit as it is for the edification of the group listening.
- In time, slowly help your worker become involved in some meaningful level of ministry.
- Consider the specific needs of the various family members or single adult.

Go over the For Your Personal Involvement section.

❑ Review any articles on the subject of re-entry.

❑ Hear the real stories of re-entry given by returned missionaries.

❑ Develop a plan for educating church members on this area of support.

Pray for those who have made the commitment to be a part of their missionary's Re-entry Support Team. Pray for those who have not yet made a decision regarding any area of support.

For Further Action

❑ Obtain materials used by various international corporations when they bring their employees home. Incorporate transferable material to your programme of re-entry.

❑ In the opening chapter of this book, we related Beth's story in which she was so distraught by her lack of re-entry support that she chose to take her own life. By God's mercy, that plan was thwarted. Unfortunately, there are other less final but equally serious forms of 'suicide' that may require professional help. If it appears that a returning missionary is not responding to the care you are able to provide, there are groups equipped to help.

❑ There may be members of your fellowship who would like to participate in a broader hospitality ministry to missionaries.

Also, most missionary societies are looking for senders willing to open their homes in hospitality to returning missionaries. One such society is Wycliffe Bible Translators, Horsleys Green, Stokenchurch, High Wycombe, Buchs.

Chapter Eight: Your Part in the Big Picture
After prayer, summarize the chapter:

❑ Leaders in the global Christian community are taking bold, dynamic steps to mobilize and deploy thousands of new missionaries to reach the unreached.

❑ God is doing a mighty work among the nations. Yet about half of the earth's population lives beyond a simple, culturally relevant presentation of the Gospel.

❑ Most of the world's 12,000 unreached people groups—in 3000 clusters live in a geographic region called the 10/40 Window.

❑ Until recently, very little has been done to target these people. In fact, today only about 8% of the world's missionary force is working among unreached peoples.

❑ They can be reached by a two-pronged attack:

1) Send thousands of 'Timothys' to teach Third World nationals the word in such a way that they will teach others. God is sovereignly raising up thousands of new Third World nationals to go as missionaries to the unreached.

2) Identify, mobilize, train and deploy thousands of 'Paulinebold' teams to penetrate these final frontiers of unreached peoples.

❑ The Christian community has the resources to see this mission accomplished by the year 2000.

❑ As part of this worldwide move, we can actively serve as senders in the six areas of support as they relate to reaching the unreached.

Go over the For Your Personal Involvement section:

❑ Focus on that most critical question Mordecai gave to Esther: 'Who knows but that you have come to royal position for such a time as this?' Relate and discuss other Scriptures that lay a responsibility for action on us to participate in God's Great

Commission (Genesis 12:1–3; Isaiah 6:8; John 20:21; Matthew 28:18–20; Mark 16:15; James 1:22).

Pray as various people share global breakthroughs on what God is doing to reach every people.

For Further Action

❑ Contact your nearest OM office (see pages 196 f. for address) and learn how you can take responsibility before God to be a partner with Operation Mobilization in reaching the unreached.

Resources

Books for Further Study

These books are available from 1) your local Christian bookstore, 2) the publisher listed, or 3) STL Order Department, PO Box 300, Carlisle, Cumbria CA3 0QS. Tel. 0800-282728 Fax. 0800-282530

Chapter Two, Moral Support

From Jerusalem to Irian Jaya: A Biographical History of Christian Missions, Ruth Tucker (Zondervan)

Shadow of the Almighty: The Life and Testament of Jim Elliot, Elisabeth Elliot (OM Publishing)

Chasing the Dragon, Jackie Pullinger (Hodder & Stoughton)

Bruchko, Bruce Olson (New Wine Press)

Vanya, Myrna Grant (Kingsway Publications)

I Dared to Call Him Father, Bilquis Sheikh (Kingsway Publications)

Eternity in Their Hearts, Don Richardson (Regal Books)

Chapter Four, Financial Support

Living More With Less, Doris Janzen Longacre (Herald Press)

Out of the Saltshaker and into the World, Rebecca Pippert (InterVarsity Press)

Tentmakers Speak Out, Don Hamilton (TMQ Research)

The Support-Raising Handbook, Brian Rust and Barry McLeish (InterVarsity Press)

'*Making Yours a Wartime, Not a Peacetime, Lifestyle,*' Ralph D. Winter (William Carey Library)

Chapter Five, Prayer Support

Touch the World Through Prayer, Wesley Duewel (Zondervan)

Destined for the Throne, Paul Billheimer (Christian Literature Crusade)

This Present Darkness, Frank Peretti (Crossway Books)

Piercing the Darkness, Frank Peretti (Crossway Books)

The Discovery of Genesis, C.H. Kang and Ethel R. Nelson (Concordia)

God's Chosen Fast, Arthur Wallis (CLC)

Operation World, Patrick J. Johnstone (OM Publishing)

Chapter Six, Communication Support

We Really Do Need to Listen, Reuben Welch (Impact Books)

Chapter Seven, Re-entry Support

Honourably Wounded, Marjory Foyle (MARC Europe)
Re-entry, John Dawson (YWAM)

Chapter Eight, Your Part in the Big Picture

Destination 2000, Bob Sjogren (Frontiers)

Our Globe and How to Reach It, David Barrett and Todd Johnson (New Hope)

The Christless Nations, J.M. Thoburn (Hunt & Eaton)

Asian Church Today, Alfred C.H. Yeo, editor (EFA)

———————

Mission Vision Resources
Introduction

A Sender needs to be equipped in three different areas:

- to have a clear understanding of God's global plan throughout history to reconcile all nations to himself, and the challenges involved in achieving this
- to grow and develop in their role as Senders
- to know how to mobilize others into involvement in world mission.

God's global plan

God's Mission: Healing the Nations, David Burnett (Paternoster)

Catch the Vision 2000 (See below, p. 222.)

Why Bother With Mission?, Steve Gaukroger (IVP.)

Other Books

No Turning Back, George Verwer. (OM Publishing) He challenges Christians to rededication, presents the disciple's weapons, teaches how to press on when the going gets tough, and shows a way to a life of love in action.

Revolution of Love, George Verwer. (OM Publishing) His *Revolution of Love* has been used to point men and women to the central theme of the Christian life for over 25 years. This is an updated edition which is joined by more recent messages on spiritual balance, the Holy Spirit, the lordship of Christ, self-acceptance, and world missions today.

Hunger For Reality, George Verwer. (OM Publishing) No one can say that we Christians are spiritually starved. Through the care and faithfulness of God's servants, we are spiritually fed, taught, encouraged, pampered, stimulated, supported and nursed along. Yet we know very well, if we are honest, that this has had too little effect on our lives.

Literature Evangelism, George Verwer. (OM Publishing) If you want to know what literature can do in the lives of people and how to do it, try this book.

The Calvary Road, Roy Hession. (Christian Literature Crusade) George Verwer says, 'This is one of the books that made the greatest impact on me as a young Christian, and in the world of Operation Mobilization around the world. We felt the message of this book was so important that it has been required reading for all who unite with us. Without this vital message, disunity and confusion so easily come into our lives and the work of God. I would recommend every believer read this book.'

What in the World is God Doing? Martin Goldsmith. (Monarch) This book discusses: Is the Church really growing worldwide? Where are people responding most eagerly? Is the West 'falling away' as fast as the statistics suggest? Are global figures *reliable? This book does far more than provide information; it is a call to action.*

Messiah Now! David Zeidan. (OM Publishing) This book contains ten true stories from modern day Israel of men and women who have met Yeshua.

The Covenant with the Jews, Walter Riggans. (Monarch) God once made a covenant with the Jews. Has he abandoned his promises in favour of the church? The church has a shameful history of anti-semitism. Is this because Christians think of themselves as the inheritors of God's favour? Are the Messianic Jews, who remain culturally Jewish but accept Jesus as their Messiah, the key to the situation? (See also *Whose Promised Land?* Colin Chapman-Lion)

The Spirit of Hinduism, David Burnett. (Monarch) Over the past century Hinduism has reached into many parts of the West. Ideas with sources in Hinduism are closely associated with the rise of the New Age Movement. As Western materialism fails to meet human aspirations, Hinduism is becoming increasingly influential.

David Burnett's meticulously researched volume describes in detail the history of Hinduism and its principal strands of thought. Karma, reincarnation, Hindu gods, Krishna and Siva, yoga, tantrism, the place of gurus: the complex way of life is set out and sign posted. 'The metaphor of a jungle is an apt one for Hindu thought,' Burnett observes. 'It has grown like a forest. Old ideas have not been discarded, but new ideas have been embraced and mixed in many varied ways.'

This informative book will provide guidance for ministers in areas with a high Asian population and will offer an indispensable resource to missionaries.

The Unseen Face of Islam, Bill Musk. (Monarch) 'This book is about weary and burdened human beings,' writes Dr. Musk. 'The masses of Muslims live today at two levels. Beneath a veneer of conformity to a major world faith, ordinary Muslims express deep needs in, their daily living.'

In Part I ten major themes are introduced by a series of short stories, based on actual experience. In Part II Dr. Musk investigates popular Islam in greater depth, showing how Christians can share their faith more fruitfully and pray with understanding. Only a power encounter with the risen Christ will meet the real needs of Muslims today. (Monarch)

Passionate Believing, Bill Musk. (Monarch) *Passionate Believing* has three sections. First, Dr. Musk introduces Islamic fundamentalism, explaining how, from a Muslim perspective, life should be organized.

Part Two presents, in details, three developing models of fundamentalism, as expressed in Pakistan, Egypt and Iran.

The third—and most disturbing—section evaluates fundamentalism in its Muslim and Christian forms. Why do the ayatollahs have such power? How have Western Christians retreated from confrontation with humanist and pagan forces? Should Muslims adopt Western values? If the differences between Christianity and Islam revolve around the Person of Jesus, how does Christ require Christians to challenge the faithlessness and corruption of much of Western culture? (Monarch)

Sadhu Sundar Singh, Phyllis Thompson. (OM Publishing) Barely hours before he intended to take his own life, the young Sundar Singh had a dramatic vision of Jesus Christ. Immediately, the emptiness and despair that had filled his heart was lifted and the search for inner peace was over.

Despite opposition and rejection at home, he knew that he had to share his faith throughout the towns and villages of India, and beyond into the dangerous mountain regions of Tibet.

What better way than to put on the robes of a sadhu, and to take to the road with no guarantee of food or shelter, but with a passionate desire to live as his Master had done before him?

Islam and Christian Witness, Martin Goldsmith. (OM Publishing) This book offers a clear perspective of the two cultures. Goldsmith explores the changing role of the Muslim faith, examines its central beliefs, discusses areas of agreement and disagreement between Christianity and Islam, and explains how Christians can present the Gospel to Muslims.

Into the Light, Steven Masood. (OM Publishing) As a boy Steven wanted to be a faithful Muslim. He studied the Qur'an. He listened to his teachers. He even tested his faith by trying to walk on water! But something denied him satisfaction, and so he set out on the long and often hard journey to truth-truth at any cost. He tells the story of that journey in a warm and personal way that will appeal to readers of all ages and backgrounds.

Growing as a Sender

By reading and acting upon the contents of this book, you are already growing into the role of a Sender.

Those who want to consider how else they can encourage their church to take its role of Sending seriously might want to consider the 'Serving as Senders' course, run by EQUIP.

This one-day course is run twice each year at Bawtry Hall, near Doncaster, and can also be run 'on location', in towns and cities across the UK.

For more information about the 'Serving as Senders' course, contact Tony Horsfall, EQUIP, Bawtry Hall, Bawtry, Doncaster, DN10 6JN (tel. 01302 710020).

Mobilizing others into world mission involvement

The best way to be a Sender is not only to support those who have already gone, but also to mobilize and send a new generation of missionaries out into God's world. The following resources will help you to do just that.

First check with your church, denomination, or mission agency, for resources and personnel who will work with you to fulfil your vision to be a Sender.

Second, check out the following generic missions-mobilizing materials:

"Why Bother With Mission?"
A book, study guide and video for house groups. This seven-week study pack is designed for those who have little or no

interest in or commitment to world mission, and shows just why we should still 'bother with mission.'

Contact IVP on 0115 978 1054, or ask at your local Christian bookshop.

"Catch the Vision 2000"
This book and study guide sets out God's heart for the nations over 12 chapters. Packed with information and ideas about how you and your church can effectively impact an unreached people group. The book is available through your local Christian bookshop, and the study guide is obtainable by calling Win Our Nations on 01799 501417.

"Serious Prayer"
This book and video is a short study programme designed for youth leaders and youth (ages 15–19), and includes a section on praying for world mission. A high quality production, published by Scripture Union.

"Mission in Action"
A 10-session, Bible-based resource for youth groups, produced jointly by CPAS and Covenanters, with guidance on opportunities for service. Available by calling 0161 474 1262 (Covenanters) or 01926 334242 (CPAS).

"God's Big Plan"
A Bible study pack which looks at God's eternal plan as it unfolds from Genesis to Revelation, in 6 studies! Available from INTERSERVE on 0171 735 8227.

"Perspectives on the World Christian Movement"
I am in God's family. What is the family business? The Perspectives course seeks to answer this question, and in doing so has raised up a whole new generation of missionaries in both the USA and New Zealand.

This 12-lesson intensive study programme has re- oriented the life direction of thousands of individuals, towards reaching the unreached peoples of the world. Local courses are run in churches, towns and cities across the UK. More information from the UK Perspectives office on 01582 463302.

''Adopt-a-People''

Once your church is mobilized to fulfil its biblical role of Sending, then focus its attention on one part of the world, or better still, one unreached people group. Pray for this people, send a prayer team to visit them, support any mission agencies which work among them, or if there are none currently doing so, ask the agencies you support what strategy they are follow-ing to ensure a church- planting team is established among them.

For more information on the Adopt-a-People programme, con-tact the Evangelical Missionary Alliance, Whitefield House, 186 Kennington Park Road, London, SE11 4BT.

Ministries available through Emmaus Road, International

ACTS Video/Audio Training Tapes

Prepare for Battle Lessons in Spiritual Warfare—This 9-hour video or audio training tapes programme comes with 19 pages of Student Notes and Assignments and a Study Guide for Groups or Individuals.

Building Your Support Team—This 2-hour, 20 minute audio training tape is the counterpart of the book, *Serving as Senders*, instructing the missionary in how to develop relationships in the six areas of support.

Solutions to Culture Stress—This 4-hour video training tape helps prepare a short-term missionary for the culture stress of going overseas and returning home.

Publications

Critical Issues in Cross-Cultural Ministry is a bi-monthly bulletin on vital missions topics. The themes of the issues revolve on a two-year cycle. Available back issues include:

Series I: *Mobilizing Your Church*

Series II: *For Those Who Go*

Series III: *Serving As Senders*

Series IV: *Internationals Who Live Among Us*

SERVING AS SENDERS: How to Care for Your Missionaries—While They are Preparing to Go, While They are on the Field, and When They Return Home.

Seminars

Nothing GOOD Just Happens! Seminar—This is an intense, 21-hour seminar to train church missions leadership in how seminar to train church missions leadership in how to mobilize their fellowship in cross-cultural outreach ministry.

For Those Who Go Seminar—The sessions of this seminar help the potential cross-cultural worker look beyond the 'romance' of missions and to deal with some very practical issues of going.

Serving as Senders Seminar—The lessons of the book, *Serving as Senders*, are presented in a 6-hour seminar format.

ACTS Training Courses

ACTS Team Orientation—2–10 hours of cultural, interpersonal relationship and spiritual warfare training for short-term teams.

ACTS Boot Camp—One week of cultural, interpersonal relationship and spiritual warfare training for those serving up to six months.

ACTS 29 Training Course—An intensive 12-week immersion in a second culture to learn how to live and minister in other cultures. The courses include cultural adaptation, language acquisition, interpersonal relationships, spiritual warfare and how to remove from the gospel and the teachings of Christ Western cultural accretions. This field training incorporates classroom study and community experience with living in the home of a national.

Mini-ACTS 29 Training Course—A 4-week modified schedule of the 12-week Course.

ACTS Ministry Trips

Four three-week trips are scheduled each year. Pre-field training, a 'hands-on' ministry trip, and follow-up with individual participants helps church leaders develop a consistent involvement in missions.

Speakers Bureau

Neal and Yvonne Pirolo, and associates of Emmaus Road, are available as speakers on a variety of subjects, all challenging to a personal involvement in cross-cultural outreach ministry.

For more information on these or other developing resources to equip you and your church for cross-cultural ministry, contact:

Emmaus Road, International
7150 Tanner Court
San Diego CA 92111 USA
619/292-7020